KIDDING Around®

NASHVILLE

WHAT TO DO, WHERE TO GO, AND HOW TO HAVE FUN IN NASHVILLE

by Tracy Barrett

John Muir Publications
Santa Fe, New Mexico

Dedicated to my research staff, Laura Beth and Patrick

John Muir Publications,
P.O. Box 613, Santa Fe, NM 87504

Printed in the United States of America
First edition. First printing March 1998

ISBN 1-56261-373-1

Editors Krista Lyons-Gould, Kristin Shahane,
Lizann Flatt
Graphics Editors Tom Gaukel, Heather Pool
Production Marie J. T. Vigil, Nikki Rooker
Cover Design Caroline Van Remortel
Typesetting Kathy Sparkes
Illustrations Stacy Venturi-Pickett
Maps Susan Harrison
Activities Kristin Shahane, Bobi Martin
Printer Hi-Liter Graphics
Cover Photo © 1998 Byron Jorjorian
Back Cover Photo S.D. Grace/Nashville Metros

Kidding Around is a registered trademark of
John Muir Publications.

Distributed to the book trade by
Publishers Group West
Emeryville, California

About the Author:
Tracy Barrett is married to a native of Nashville, and has herself
lived in Nashville since 1984. She teaches at Vanderbilt
University. *Kidding Around Nashville* is her sixth children's book.
Tracy has two children, Laura Beth age 13, and Patrick age 10.

C O N T E N T S

COLOR THE ROUTE
FROM YOUR HOMETOWN TO NASHVILLE

If you're flying, color the states you'll fly over.
If you're driving, color the states you'll drive through.
If you live in Nashville or Tennessee, color the states you have visited.

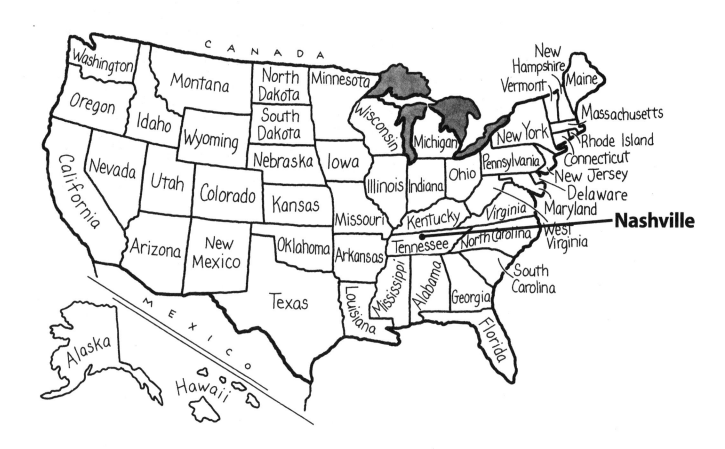

WELCOME TO NASHVILLE!

HOME TO THE GRAND OLE OPRY, world-famous country music stars, and the Fisk Jubilee Singers, Nashville is known all over the world as "Music City, U.S.A." Some people call it "Twangtown." To truckers, Nashville is "Guitar Town." The city's many banks and insurance companies have led to the nickname "Wall Street of the South."

Visitors love this city of many nicknames. Exciting museums, bustling sports attractions, lively outdoor activities, great restaurants, and hands-on historical sites are here for travelers of all ages. Nashville is a great place to explore!

↥ **Nashville's Waterfront Park**

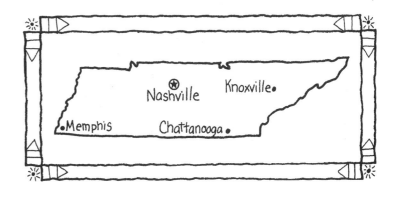

THE FIRST TENNESSEANS

The first people came to middle Tennessee about 11,000 years ago to hunt mastodons (huge, mammoth-like creatures), bears, and other animals. Over time, several different Native American tribes lived and hunted in the area. The Cherokee, who called themselves "Ani-Yunwiya," which means the "real people," were the largest group. The Cherokee divided each of their tribes into seven clans, or family groups. They had large villages with many houses.

↥ **Andrew Jackson was the seventh President of the United States.**

EUROPEAN SETTLERS

Explorers from European countries were attracted to the area by its beauty as well as by the good hunting and farmland. Fort Nashborough, the area's first permanent settlement, was founded in 1779 by James Robertson and John Donelson.

From the start, the settlers and the Native Americans had trouble getting along. The most important peacemaker was Nancy Ward, a Cherokee leader who said, "Our cry is all for peace." Unfortunately, disagreements between the two groups continued. In 1830, President Andrew Jackson, a Tennessee native, ordered that all Cherokee in the southeastern United States had to move to Oklahoma. About one-quarter of the Indians died on this trip. The sadness felt by the Indians gave the path the name "The Trail of Tears."

Greater Nashville

THE CIVIL WAR

When the Civil War first broke out, Tennessee chose to stay in the Union (the group of states loyal to the United States), but later joined the Confederacy (the group of states that wanted to set up a separate country). The Union captured Nashville in 1862. The last important battle in Tennessee was the Battle of Nashville, in December 1864. In this battle, the Confederacy failed to recapture the city. At Fort Negley and on top of Shy's Hill, you can still see where Civil War soldiers took shelter in ditches carved into the earth. Visitors to these areas sometimes find bullets, knives, and pieces of guns from the Civil War.

🡡 **Civil War encampment re-created in the Tennessee State Museum.**

NASHVILLE RISES

The Civil War destroyed much of Tennessee, ruining its farms and cities. But the state was quick to rebuild. The population of Tennessee doubled between 1860 and 1880. Nashville was a river port, so it became an important center of trade.

During the Great Depression of the 1930s, Tennessee suffered terribly. Many people didn't have jobs and were very poor. The Tennessee Valley Authority (TVA) was created to provide jobs and to bring electricity to the rural, or outlying, parts of the state. The TVA and the Army Corps of Engineers built dams on many of the rivers. These dams formed lakes. Two of them, Old Hickory Lake and Percy Priest Lake, are near Nashville and now provide fishing, boating, and swimming.

The nation's longest-running radio show, the *Grand Ole Opry*, started broadcasting from Nashville in 1925. Because of this show, Nashville quickly became the center of the country music industry.

⇑ **The Nashville Riverfront in the 1850s**

Nashville's nickname of "Music City" doesn't come from the country music industry, but from the famous Fisk Jubilee Singers, a chorus from Nashville's historically black Fisk University.

NASHVILLIANS IN THE NEWS

If you think that a lot of famous country music stars live in Nashville, you're right! Garth Brooks, Alan Jackson, Reba McEntire, and other stars make their homes in or near Music City. If you're a country music fan, be sure to sign up for one of the tours featuring the homes of these stars.

Nashville and the surrounding area are also home to some well-known politicians. Vice president of the United States Al Gore Jr. is from nearby Carthage. Lamar Alexander, who was President Reagan's secretary of education and has run for president himself, lived in Nashville while he was governor of Tennessee.

If you've ever visited the Chicago Art Institute, the Hirshhorn Museum and Sculpture Garden in Washington, D.C., or the Museum of Modern Art in New York, you've probably seen the sculptures by artist Red Grooms. Grooms was born and raised in Nashville. Be sure to watch the wall as you go down the escalator at the Tennessee State Museum. That's where Red Grooms painted an escalator of the future showing the people taking off into outer space as they reach the bottom. More of his art is at the Fine Arts Center at Cheekwood.

⇑ **Country music star, Reba McEntire**

For one of the nation's most complete collections of photographs of country music stars, check out the wall of the post office at 2002 Acklen Avenue.

MUSIC CITY U.S.A. WORD SEARCH

Hidden in this word search are some things you might see or do in Nashville. Search for words vertically, horizontally, and diagonally. Can you find all 12 words? The first word has been found for you.

Word Box

banks	souvenirs	restaurants
Opryland	churches	colleges
parks	country music	forts
art	sports	theater

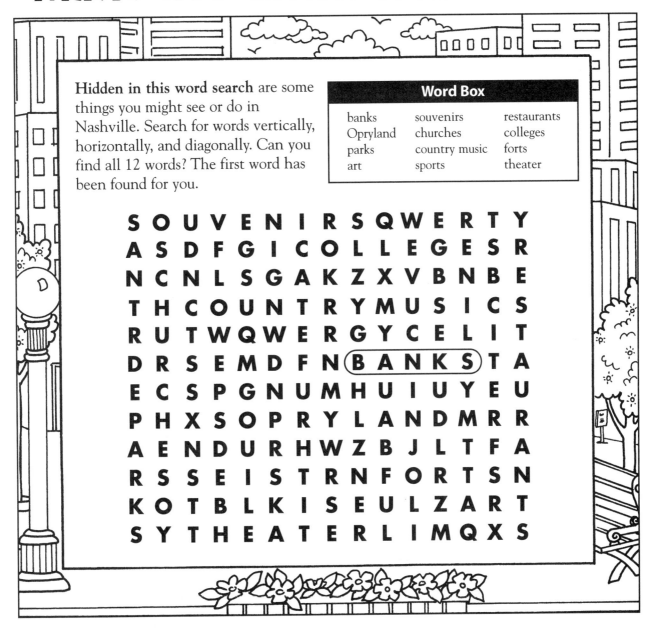

```
S O U V E N I R S Q W E R T Y
A S D F G I C O L L E G E S R
N C N L S G A K Z X V B N B E
T H C O U N T R Y M U S I C S
R U T W Q W E R G Y C E L I T
D R S E M D F N B A N K S T A
E C S P G N U M H U I U Y E U
P H X S O P R Y L A N D M R R
A E N D U R H W Z B J L T F A
R S S E I S T R N F O R T S N
K O T B L K I S E U L Z A R T
S Y T H E A T E R L I M Q X S
```

MILD AND GREEN

Nashville gets about 47 inches of rain a year. Although it can get cold in the winter, it rarely snows. The summer is long, hot, and humid. Spring and fall are long seasons in Nashville, and both are beautiful. The rainfall and mild climate make the area very green. Nashvillians take pride in their gardens and plant many flowers.

⇑ **Lots of rain makes Tennessee beautiful and green.**

camera
backpack
bathing suit
map
windbreaker
sunglasses
sweatshirt
jeans
snack
comfortable walking shoes
cap
water bottle
important numbers and addresses
rain gear
pocket change
shorts

Here are some ideas of what to take when you're out exploring Nashville!

GETTING AROUND MUSIC CITY

Tourists love Nashville. In fact, more bus loads of tourists go to Nashville than to any other city in the U.S. Nashville's streets are busy, but the city is easy to get around because three interstates cut right through it. The major streets are arranged like spokes on a wheel. So some streets that are close together when you're downtown are far apart on the outskirts of town.

⇡ **Ride the *General Jackson* showboat.**

There are several good ways to see the city. You can ride in one of the open-air buses operated by the Nashville Trolley Company or go on a horse-and-buggy tour of downtown. Walking tours are also available. You can see the city's historic sights as you stroll down the streets. For a view of Nashville from the water, take a ride on the *General Jackson*, the world's largest showboat, and enjoy dinner and entertainment. Many companies offer bus tours of the city. Some of them will guide you through the history of country music, and some will show you the homes of famous country stars.

Many of the main streets in Nashville started out as buffalo and deer paths.

HIDDEN MESSAGE

What might the trolley conductor say to you when it's time to get on?

The answer is hidden in the box below. To find it, cross out all the J's, P's, W's, Xs, and Z's. The letters remaining spell the answer to this riddle!

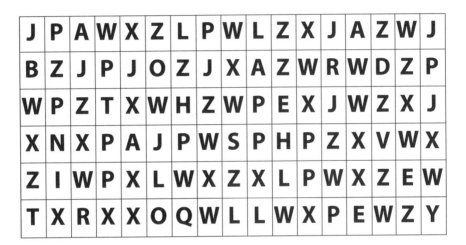

J	P	A	W	X	Z	L	P	W	L	Z	X	J	A	Z	W	J
B	Z	J	P	J	O	Z	J	X	A	Z	W	R	W	D	Z	P
W	P	Z	T	X	W	H	Z	W	P	E	X	J	W	Z	X	J
X	N	X	P	A	J	P	W	S	P	H	P	Z	X	V	W	X
Z	I	W	P	X	L	W	X	Z	X	L	P	W	X	Z	E	W
T	X	R	X	X	O	Q	W	L	L	W	X	P	E	W	Z	Y

Write the hidden message below:

 PARKS AND THE GREAT OUTDOORS

THE PEOPLE OF NASHVILLE LOVE BEING outdoors. The warm weather and beautiful countryside make it the perfect place for everyone to enjoy nature. Percy Priest and Old Hickory Lakes are great spots for swimming, fishing, and boating. Montgomery Bell State Park is a quiet forest within easy reach of downtown Nashville.

If you don't want to leave the city, you won't have any trouble finding a green place with trees and animals. Nashvillians have filled their city with parks so they never have to go very far to get to back to nature. Whether you're looking for a great playground, a duck pond, a piece of history, tennis courts, or a locomotive to climb on, Nashville has a park for you.

↥ **Some Nashvillians sail on Percy Priest Lake.**

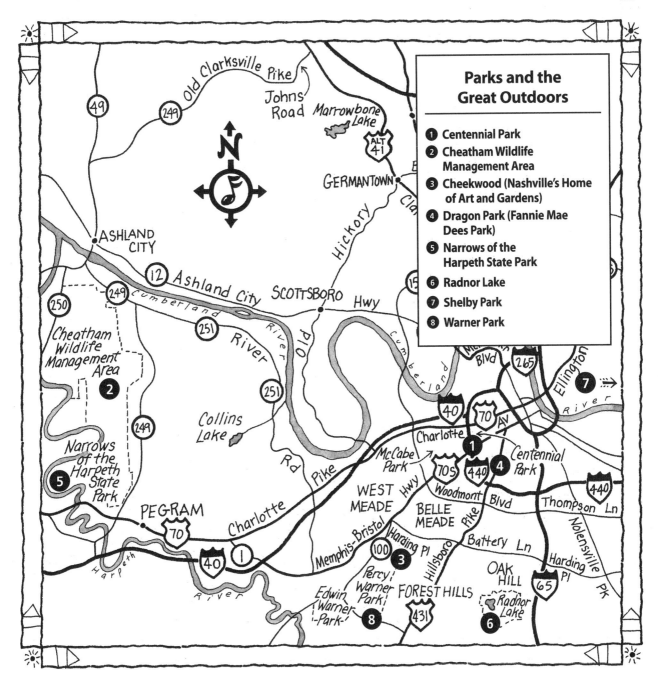

Parks and the Great Outdoors

1. Centennial Park
2. Cheatham Wildlife Management Area
3. Cheekwood (Nashville's Home of Art and Gardens)
4. Dragon Park (Fannie Mae Dees Park)
5. Narrows of the Harpeth State Park
6. Radnor Lake
7. Shelby Park
8. Warner Park

CENTENNIAL PARK

Centennial Park contains Nashville's most famous monument—the world's only full-sized copy of the famous Parthenon in Athens, Greece. Nashville's Parthenon was built to celebrate the state's one-hundredth birthday in 1896. Local artist Alan LeQuire's 42-foot statue of the Greek goddess Athena is in the main room inside the Parthenon. It's the largest indoor sculpture in the western world.

Centennial Park stretches for 132 acres and includes a playground, tennis courts, picnic areas, and large fields. If you like trains, or if you just like to climb, there's an old locomotive parked near the playground. Kids love it! The Nashville Symphony gives free concerts here, and Centennial Park is also home to the Nashville Shakespeare Festival.

⇑ **Visit Nashville's famous Parthenon in Centennial Park.**

A local McDonald's restaurant gave its flagpole to be used as Athena's spear.

ATHENA ON THE LOOSE

Without telling anyone what you're doing, ask for a word to fill in each blank. For example, "Give me an action word." When all the blanks are filled in, read the story out loud. One of the blanks has been filled in for you.

Athena was ____happy____ with being stuck inside the Parthenon. "I'm
                 emotion

_____ outside in the park," she decided.
action word

"_____!" she said happily. "The grass is so _____ and
       exclamation   color

the trees are so _____." Just then she heard a band playing.
                  describing word

Athena grabbed her _____ and _____ to the band.
                        thing   action word

"I've always wanted to lead a _____!"
                                  thing

DRAGON PARK

A work of art is the centerpiece of **Fannie Mae Dees Park**, locally known as the "Dragon Park." The park's two sculptures of an adult sea serpent and its baby wind their way through the playground. The dragons were made by artist Pedro Silva and the people of the community in 1981. The sculptures are covered with glittery mosaics, which are scenes and pictures made from thousands of tiny pieces of glass and pottery glued together. If you look closely at the mosaics, you can see Mickey Mouse, astronauts, people, flowers, fish, mermaids, Nashville landmarks, and much more. You can climb on the sculptures, explore a long tunnel running through a hill, and play on the swing sets.

Look for the artists' signatures in mosaic on the larger sea serpent.

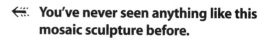

←:: **You've never seen anything like this mosaic sculpture before.**

WHAT'S THE DIFFERENCE?

Can you find the differences in these two scenes of the Dragon Park?
Look for at least 15 differences.

SHELBY PARK

⇡ **How many ducks and geese can you count on the pond?**

One of Nashville's best-kept secrets is Shelby Park, tucked among quiet residential streets in East Nashville. The people who live nearby treasure the park for its rolling, hilly landscape, duckpond, golf course, and most of all its playgrounds. The park also has picnic tables, baseball diamonds, and a boat ramp where people can set off on a day of fishing or exploring the Cumberland River.

Shelby Park attracts families. You can see children walking their dogs and hear birthdays being celebrated with friends. Almost any day of the week you can see grandparents with their grandchildren feeding the ducks and geese in the pond or teaching their grandchildren how to fish. Neighborhood softball and baseball teams practice and play in the well-maintained diamonds. But you don't have to be an East Nashvillian to enjoy Shelby Park—visitors are welcome too.

CONNECT THE DOTS

Parks are great places for exercise. Who do you think is getting the most exercise in this picture?

CHEEKWOOD

Cheekwood, Nashville's Home of Art and Gardens, is located on 55 acres of Botanical Gardens. Trails wind through the Wildflower Garden where you can see many of the beautiful plants native to Tennessee and other parts of the southeastern United States. In the Herb Garden, you will notice signs in both braille and English that invite you to touch and smell the plants as well as look at them. Don't skip the Japanese Garden, where you walk through a bamboo grove and past Japanese sculptures to a peaceful wooden shelter with a view of a miniature lake. Instead of water, this lake is made of tiny pebbles raked in a design to look like ripples of water. New to Cheekwood in 1998: an interactive Woodland Sculpture Trail and Learning Center.

Explore one of Cheekwood's garden trails.

Cheekwood was named when its owner, Mr. Leslie Cheek, married Miss Mable Wood. They combined their last names to come up with the name for the house.

CROSSWORD FUN

There are lots of things to see and do in a garden. Solve this crossword by figuring out the clues or completing the sentences. If you need some help, use the clue box.

Across

2. Pieces of land surrounded by water.
4. On your mark, get set, _____!
6. You can plant flowers, herbs, or vegetables in these.
7. The opposite of girl.
8. The herb garden has signs in braille and _____.

Down

1. You'll see lots of these at the gardens.
2. The opposite of out.
3. Look for these to learn what kind of flower you're looking at.
5. Basil is an _____ you can grow in your garden.
6. Look for the bamboo _____ in the Japanese garden.

Clue Box

gardens	in	boy
islands	signs	grove
flowers	go	
English	herb	

WARNER PARKS

If you'd like to learn how to build a bird feeder, identify trees, listen to Native American campfire stories, hike under the full moon, garden, or identify insect sounds, you should visit Warner Parks.

Here you will also find 12 miles of nature trails—some short and easy and some long and hilly. There are separate paths for people on horseback or for people riding bikes. Picnic tables are scattered throughout the park. Get an adult to help you build a fire in the fireplace in one of the shelters and cook a meal or roast some marshmallows. There are also playgrounds and a model airplane field.

Check in at the nature center for a trail map and a schedule of events.

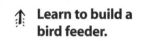

⇞ **Learn to build a bird feeder.**

Warner Parks were named for brothers Percy and Edwin Warner, two early Nashville conservationists who worked to protect the environment.

⇞ **Gardening is fun at Warner Park Nature Center.**

WHAT'S IN COMMON

Each of these birdhouses has something in common with the two others in the same row. For example, there is a bird on each house in the middle row of houses. Draw lines through each row and describe what the houses in that row have in common. Don't forget diagonals!

Disabled visitors can enjoy the park's rugged paths in one of the all-terrain wheelchairs available at the visitor center.

If you look closely, you might see turtles at Radnor Lake.

RADNOR LAKE

Radnor Lake is a favorite spot for Nashville residents and it might be a favorite spot for you, too. The lake is surrounded by a huge park so there's plenty of room to run, jump, and hike. Radnor Lake is dedicated to the protection of the environment, so hunting, fishing, picnicking, and swimming are not allowed.

Pick up a trail map at the visitor center. At the main trailhead you can also get a list of the natural wonders along the trail. As you hike, numbered posts at the side of the trail tell you what to look at. Look around and you might see snakes sunning themselves on the path, shy salamanders, and many birds. At the lake, you're likely to see Canada geese, ducks, and other water birds, as well as turtles blending in with the natural surroundings.

SALAMANDER SEARCH

Can you find all the shy salamanders hidden in this scene?
Hint: There are 19 salamanders.

PARKS NEAR NASHVILLE

The Harpeth State Park "Narrows" get their name from the fact that the Harpeth River makes such a sharp bend here that it nearly curves back in on itself. Rent a canoe and spend half a day floating down the river. Near the end of your trip, look for the tunnel that was dug through the bend to power a mill in the 1830s. When you look through the tunnel, you're seeing the area where you got into your canoe two or three hours earlier!

The Cheatham Wildlife Management Area in Ashland City is a huge preserve with more than 150 miles of back roads and trails. Hundreds of deer roam wild through the area, and several tame ones are kept in a pen at the headquarters. These deer aren't scared of humans and will allow you to feed them a treat.

⇡ **Canoe in the "Narrows" of the Harpeth River.**

More deer roam Tennessee today than were in the entire United States when Columbus came to America.

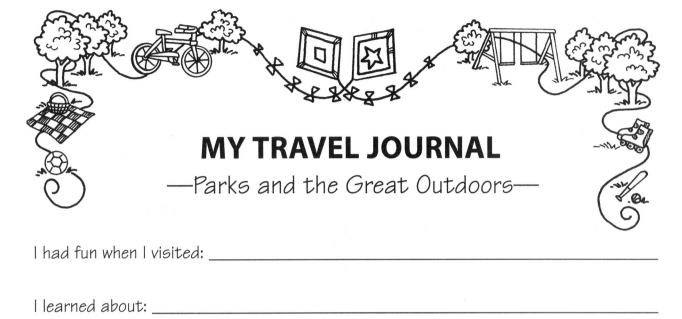

MY TRAVEL JOURNAL
—Parks and the Great Outdoors—

I had fun when I visited: _____

I learned about: _____

My favorite park was: _____

This is a picture of what I saw at a park in Nashville •••••➤

3 ANIMALS, ANIMALS

THE MANY WOODS, LAKES, AND RIVERS around Nashville are home to thousands of animals. Small mammals, such as opossums, raccoons, foxes, rabbits, and bobcats are common, and some even roam the city. There are so many deer that they are pests to farmers and homeowners whose flowers get eaten by the daring animals. Coyotes have been spotted near Nashville, and visitors to the state parks in Middle Tennessee often see black bears and occasionally a wild boar.

Birds love Tennessee's mild climate and its many trees and flowers. It's not unusual to see 15 different kinds of birds gathered around a bird feeder at one time. Cardinals, finches, martins, and the mockingbird (the Tennessee state bird) are some of the most beautiful birds you can see in town.

A young deer at Warner Park Nature Center

Animals , Animals

1 Cumberland Science Museum
2 Hohenwald Elephant Sanctuary
3 Nashville Zoo (Jungle Gym)
4 Warner Park Nature Center

WARNER PARK NATURE CENTER

Get to know the animals of Middle Tennessee with a visit to the museum of natural history at the Warner Park Nature Center. Mammals, birds, and reptiles that live in the area are on display. You'll even see a tank filled with fish that live in Tennessee. The nature center's grounds are open to visitors. Visit the small pond filled with native fish and plants, the garden blooming with local wildflowers, and the bird nesting boxes and bat boxes.

Visitors are welcome on the nature center's grounds.

The guides can tell you where you're likely to see animals hiding, but walk quietly! Wild animals are usually very shy. You can take special tours to help you learn more about nature. Sign up for a moonlight tour where you might be lucky enough to see an owl. Stop to smell the flowers on a wildflower walk. Or take a hike where you learn to tell different trees apart by looking at their bark and leaves.

WHERE DO THEY LIVE?

**By tracing the tracks of each animal,
can you discover who belongs in which den?**

CUMBERLAND SCIENCE MUSEUM

⬆ **Would you be brave enough to touch a snake?**

A good spot to get a close look at some of Tennessee's wildlife is at an animal show at the Cumberland Science Museum. You'll learn how animals' colors keep them safe from their enemies, or you might hear about different animals' favorite foods. The museum is also home to several small animals. Most of them can't live in the wild because they have been injured or were raised as pets and have forgotten how to find their own food and take care of themselves. There are opossums, raccoons, ducks, snakes, turtles, ferrets, rabbits, and more. You can touch most of the animals in the museum's show, and you may be surprised to find out that a snake is not slimy!

Don't be worried if you hear someone calling for help at the Cumberland Museum—it's just a lonely parrot who knows that people will come running when it screams, "Help! Help!"

SILLY PARROT

Without telling anyone what you're doing, ask for a word to fill in each blank. For example, "Give me an action word." When all the blanks are filled in, read the story out loud. One of the blanks has been filled in for you.

Kristina was _____ the Cumberland Science Museum. She_____
                        action word   emotion

learning about all of the animals. She especially liked the big,

____purple____ parrot. Anytime someone _____
        color   action word

past his cage he _____, "Help! Help!"
                        sound

This time he squawked so loud he lost his balance.

"_____ parrot," Kristina laughed.
    describing word

"Be careful or you'll _____ right
                            action word

into your _____!"
                thing

THE NASHVILLE ZOO

See exotic animals at the Nashville Zoo. The zoo specializes in big cats, like tigers, lions, and cheetahs. It is also home to different types of deer, red pandas, and lots of other animals. The animals are so comfortable here that some endangered species, like the beautiful clouded leopard, are breeding well and supplying other zoos with cubs.

Stop in at the petting zoo where you can play with tame animals like goats, deer, and pigs. There is also a zoo nursery, where you can see newborn animals.

The **Jungle Gym** at the zoo is the largest educational playground area for children in the United States. The best part is a gigantic wooden climbing structure. You can ride an elephant at the zoo too!

⇑ **Have you ever seen a camel up close?**

The huge Jungle Gym at the zoo was built almost entirely by community volunteers.

⇐ **The Nashville Zoo specializes in big cats, including tigers.**

CAMOUFLAGE CONFUSION

Animals who have camouflaged skin have an advantage. They are better able to blend in with their surroundings. Each of these animals has camouflaged skin but it is the wrong pattern. Color in the correct camouflage pattern on the blank animals.

THE HOHENWALD ELEPHANT SANCTUARY

Have you ever wondered what happens to circus elephants when they grow too old to perform or when they get sick or injured? The lucky ones go to the Hohenwald Elephant Sanctuary and roam free on 112 acres of land. These retired circus elephants receive medical care and food, and spend the winter in a heated barn. At the sanctuary, these friendly creatures live the way they do in the wild—with other elephants.

Since the sanctuary's main mission is to protect the endangered Asian elephant, visits are limited. But you can get a great view of these magnificent creatures because of the sanctuary's Diane Project. A trained worker films the elephants in the sanctuary, being careful not to disturb them. You can watch the elephants on a computer equipped with a phone line as they are being filmed. The pictures from the video are sent over the phone lines to your computer and appear on the screen.

⇑ **Elephants roam free on sanctuary land.**

You can check on the elephants through the sanctuary's web page on the Internet at www.elephants. com

MY TRAVEL JOURNAL
—Animals, Animals—

I had fun when I visited: _____

I learned about: _____

_____

My favorite animal was: _____

This is a picture of an animal I saw

4 LANDMARKS, SKYSCRAPERS, AND THE ARTS

FOR COUNTRY MUSIC FANS, THERE IS NO place like Nashville. But don't think that you have to love guitars to find great things to do in Nashville—there's something for everyone!

For years, businesses were having a hard time in downtown Nashville. Movie theaters and stores closed, and the streets became deserted and dirty. Finally, the mayor, businesses, and citizens came together to create a new and lively city center. Great restaurants were opened, and stores with every kind of country-music souvenir you can imagine now line the streets. Music pours out of open doors and windows. Downtown Nashville is now a bustling and lively part of the city, and it is a terrific place for you to explore!

Nashville shines at night.

Landmarks, Skyscrapers, and the Arts

1. Belmont Mansion
2. Bicentennial Mall
3. Downtown Presbyterian Church
4. Ryman Auditorium
5. Tennessee State Capitol
6. Union Station

THE RYMAN AUDITORIUM

The most famous building in downtown Nashville is the Ryman Auditorium. It was originally built as a religious meeting hall in 1892. For decades, its halls rang with the sounds of sermons as listeners crowded into the wooden pews, or benches. Eventually, musicians replaced the preachers. The Ryman is famous because it was the original home of the *Grand Ole Opry*, the country's longest-running live radio show. The Ryman was restored in 1994, and it still looks the same inside and out as it did when it housed the Opry, in the 1940s through 1970s.

When concerts are not being performed, you can go up on stage. A microphone is set up just where Loretta Lynn, Johnny Cash, Minnie Pearl, Chet Atkins, and all the other stars of country music used to perform.

⇑ **The famous Ryman Auditorium**

The Ryman isn't big enough to hold all the country fans who come to Nashville these days, so the Opry has moved across the river to Opryland.

WHAT'S THE DIFFERENCE?

**These two scenes of the Grand Ole Opry might look the same, but they are not.
How many differences between the two scenes can you find?
Hint: There are at least 10 differences.**

UNION STATION

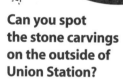

Nashville's Union Station, a huge stone train station, hasn't seen any passengers since the 1970s, but the building is far from empty. The seven-story station was built in 1900 and was restored in 1986. It is now home to a luxury hotel, restaurants, and shops. Before you go in, take a few minutes to look at the stone carvings on the outside. When you enter, go up to the fourth floor and look up three stories to the stained-glass ceiling.

The train shed next to the station was falling apart and was almost destroyed by a fire in 1996. But different groups have come together to restore the enormous building.

Can you spot the stone carvings on the outside of Union Station?

Union Station's tower had the world's first digital clock.

STAINED-GLASS MYSTERY

The stained-glass window contains a hidden picture. Use the following color code to fill in the window and discover the picture.

1=Brown, 2=Yellow, 3=Flesh Tone, 4=Green, 5=Lt. Blue, 6=Bright Blue

TENNESSEE STATE CAPITOL

For a step back in time, check out the Tennessee State Capitol. Built between 1845 and 1859, the capitol is on a hill and can be seen from most places in the city. It's best to visit the capitol during the week when all the rooms are open and you can get a guided tour. You can also take a self-guided tour.

You'll see marble statues of famous Tennesseans, including the three United States presidents from Tennessee: Andrew Johnson, Andrew Jackson, and James K. Polk. There is also a statue of Sequoyah, the Cherokee leader.

Look up when you're under the dome, and you'll see paintings on the ceiling that show different scenes from Tennessee's past. There is also a lot of history in the capitol building. You can still see a bullet hole in the stair rail where a shot was fired at two people after the Civil War.

Look for the historical bullet hole in the stair rail inside the capitol.

William Strickland, the designer of the capitol, died before the building was finished and is buried in one of its walls.

LOST IN THE CAPITOL

Henry and his sister Kate got separated from the tour group in the State Capitol. Can you help them find their way back to the group?

BICENTENNIAL MALL

The expression "the past is written in stone" comes true at one of Nashville's newest attractions, the 16-acre Bicentennial Mall State Park—not a shopping mall, but an outdoor history museum. The park will grow slowly for several years, so every time you visit, you can see something new.

You can walk on the huge stone map of Tennessee at the mall's entrance. Lights mark the locations of the larger cities, and the rivers, lakes, and major highways stand out in different shades of gray stone. Surrounding the large map are smaller maps. One shows the old Indian trails of Tennessee, and another one shows all of Tennessee's rivers and lakes.

A shiny black stone monument lists Tennessee's rivers and streams. There is a separate fountain for each river in Tennessee. You can walk down the Trail of Volunteers to the outdoor theater.

Each river fountain is a different height. The higher the fountain, the longer the river it stands for.

⇑ **Check out the fountains at the Bicentennial Mall.**

FUN WITH NASHVILLE WORDS

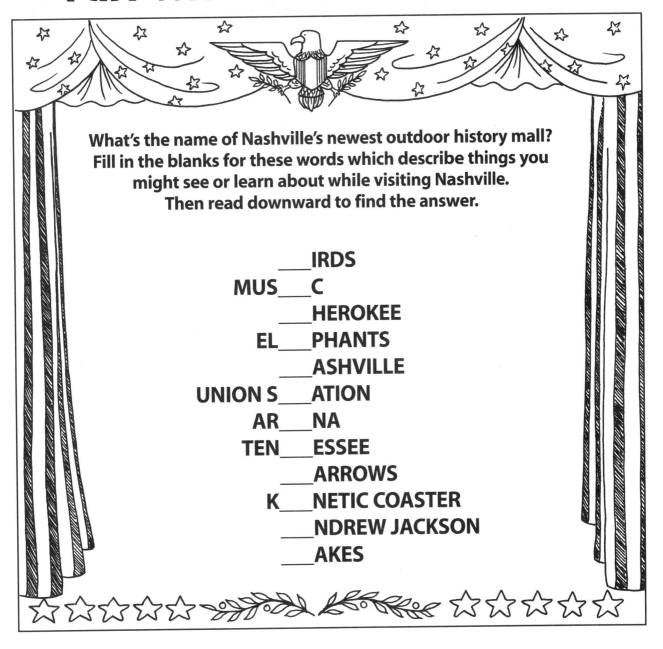

What's the name of Nashville's newest outdoor history mall?
Fill in the blanks for these words which describe things you
might see or learn about while visiting Nashville.
Then read downward to find the answer.

```
        ___IRDS
    MUS___C
        ___HEROKEE
     EL___PHANTS
        ___ASHVILLE
UNION S___ATION
     AR___NA
    TEN___ESSEE
        ___ARROWS
      K___NETIC COASTER
        ___NDREW JACKSON
        ___AKES
```

DOWNTOWN PRESBYTERIAN CHURCH

Probably the most unusual of Nashville's more than 80 churches is the Downtown Presbyterian Church. From the outside, this stone building looks like any other church. Step inside, and you'll suddenly feel like you're in ancient Egypt.

The church was built in 1849 when a style called Egyptian Revival was very popular. The designers wanted visitors to feel as though they were inside the ancient Egyptian temple of Karnak. The walls are painted to look like columns, and the stained-glass windows represent the Nile River. Each window shows a different scene of Egyptian life. In some, almost all you see is the river, but in others you can see sand dunes and palm trees. Paintings of two Egyptian snakes, the asp and the cobra, wind around the walls. Originally, the ceiling was painted blue with fluffy white clouds, but the paint has now faded to green.

⇡ **Step into Egypt when you step inside Downtown Presbyterian Church.**

HIDE AND SEEK

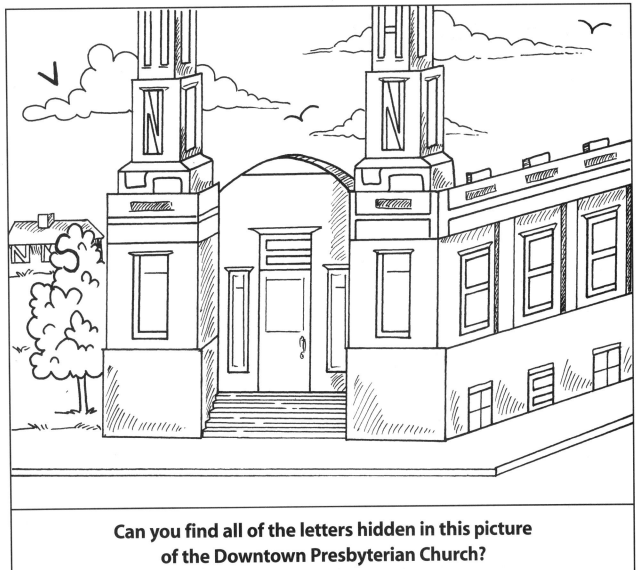

**Can you find all of the letters hidden in this picture
of the Downtown Presbyterian Church?
Hint: Where is Music City U.S.A.?**

Gas was a rarity in Adelicia Acklen's day and her use of it showed her visitors just how rich she was.

BELMONT MANSION

Nashville has produced its share of colorful characters, but Adelicia Acklen would top almost anyone's list of interesting people. She was one of the wealthiest people in the South before the Civil War, and she spent a huge amount of money on her beautiful mansion.

Adelicia Acklen's home is now part of Belmont University, but much of it appears the way it did when she lived there. Visitors are always moved by the beautiful statue of sleeping children. This statue, of pure white marble, is a memorial to two of her ten children who died at age two.

Keep your eyes open and you'll see animals everywhere. Find the Italian wolfhounds holding up the umbrella stand in the black walnut hall-tree, and the deer in the gasolier—a gas chandelier—in the library.

Winter visitors enjoy the annual "Christmas at Belmont" celebration, with the mansion decorated in nineteenth-century style.

The beautiful Belmont Mansion

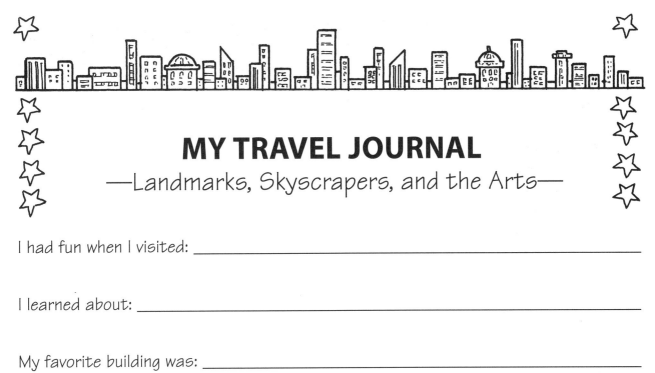

MY TRAVEL JOURNAL
—Landmarks, Skyscrapers, and the Arts—

I had fun when I visited: _____

I learned about: _____

My favorite building was: _____

This is a picture of a building I saw

 GOOD SPORTS

SPORTS OF ALL KINDS ARE POPULAR IN Nashville. Middle Tennessee is the home of the famous Tennessee walking horse, and many Nashvillians love to horseback ride. Middle Tennessee is one of the world's most popular spots for canoeing, kayaking, and other white-water sports. Hikers can stroll down easy paths or test their skill on rocky trails that lead to hidden waterfalls.

Until recently, Tennessee had no professional sports teams. But, in 1995, the Houston Oilers football team announced plans to move to Nashville and become the Tennessee Oilers. Work started immediately on a 65,000-seat stadium on the east bank of the Cumberland River. The stadium will open in 1998.

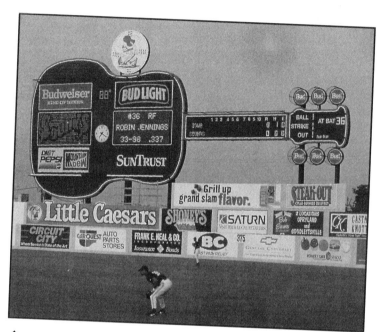

The Nashville Sounds have a guitar-shaped scoreboard.

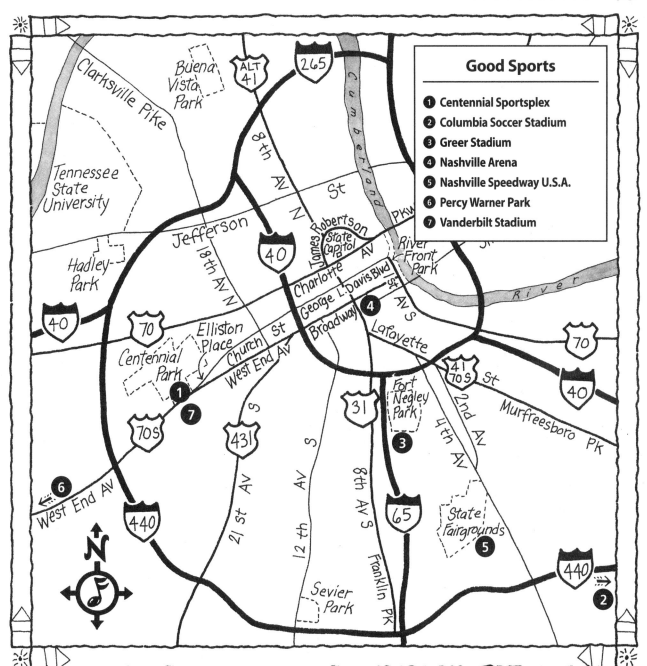

THE NASHVILLE ARENA

Visitors to Nashville's downtown have a brand-new place to hear music and watch sports and other shows. The Nashville Arena, a huge theater which seats 20,000 people, opened its doors in December 1996 with a sold-out concert by singer Amy Grant.

Nashville's first professional arena football team, the Nashville Kats, play at the arena, and different sports events are scheduled all the time. Nashville is hoping to attract a major league ice hockey team. WWF wrestling, the Harlem Globetrotters, Ohio Valley Conference basketball, monster trucks, and figure skating championships are all scheduled to take place here at different times of the year. Be sure to check out the arena's Tennessee Sports Hall of Fame, which has displays on well-known athletes from Tennessee.

⇧ **Fans meet the Nashville Kats football players at the arena.**

Many Nashvillians were disappointed when a contest to name the arena didn't lead to a more interesting name. What would you have called it?

FOOTBALL MAZE

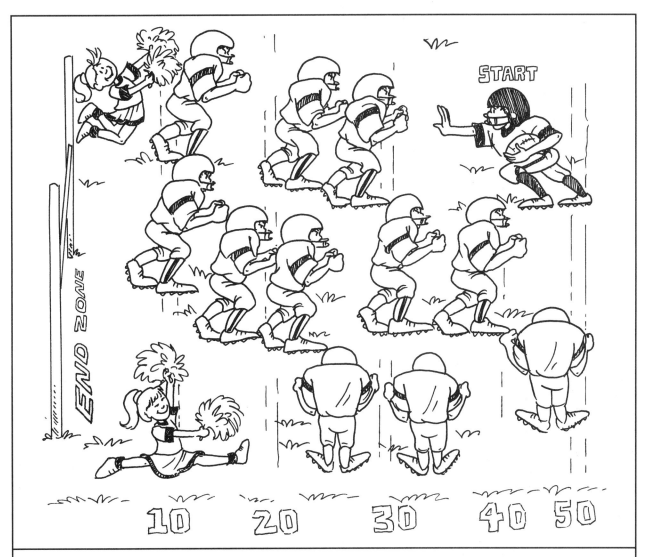

The football player with the ball needs to reach the end zone to score a touchdown. Can you help him get there?

THE NASHVILLE SOUNDS

Great baseball stars usually start in Little League and make their way through the minor leagues. If they're lucky and talented, they go from the minors to the major leagues. The best minor league teams are called "AAA." On summer nights, as many as 4,000 baseball fans watch the AAA minor league team, the Nashville Sounds, demonstrate their championship style at Greer Stadium.

The Sounds are a farm team of the Chicago White Sox, and stars like Don Mattingly, Ray Durham, James Baldwin, and Willie McGee all moved on to the majors after playing with the Sounds. Through the season, the team sponsors different giveaway nights for the fans. Occasionally, major league teams play exhibition games at Greer Stadium.

⇑ **Ozzie the cougar, is the Nashville Sounds' mascot.**

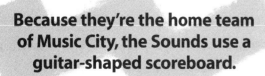

Because they're the home team of Music City, the Sounds use a guitar-shaped scoreboard.

⇑ **On Family Day, you can meet the players.**

WHAT'S THE DIFFERENCE?

These two scenes of a Nashville Sounds baseball game might look the same, but they are not. How many differences between the two scenes can you find?
Hint: There are at least 15 differences.

THE NASHVILLE KATS

Cats play in alleys, and in Nashville, the Kats play in The Alley, their nickname for the Nashville Arena. Arena football is basically the same as regular football, but it is played indoors on a field half the size of a regular football field. Although some of the rules are different, most of the action is what football fans are used to. What makes arena football especially fast and exciting is the iron man style of play; all team members except the quarterback and kicker play both offense and defense.

Adding to the excitement are the rebound nets on both ends of the field. Balls kicked or thrown too hard don't go out of bounds—they bounce back in for nonstop action.

⇡ **The Kats play in "The Alley," the Nashville Arena's nickname.**

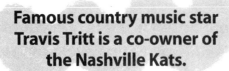

Famous country music star Travis Tritt is a co-owner of the Nashville Kats.

MATCH THE SHOES

The football players won the game and left the locker room in a hurry. Can you help the coach clean up the locker room by matching the shoes?

Foxhunters used to race their horses across fields and through woods to try to be the first to reach a steeple in a nearby town. This is where the word steeplechase came from.

THE IROQUOIS STEEPLECHASE

Howling foxhounds, riders in colorful clothes, gleaming horses from all over the world jumping over fences and hedges—are you in England? No, you're in Nashville's **Percy Warner Park**, watching the Iroquois Steeplechase!

This race is named for Iroquois, the first American horse to win the famous English Derby. Iroquois was born at Nashville's Belle Meade Stables. The Iroquois Steeplechase has been run every year since 1922.

There are lots of green fields where you can have a picnic during the race. Bring your own, or buy food from the concession stands. Rain or shine, the first race starts at 1:00 p.m., and by 4:30 p.m. six races have been run, with eight to ten horses in each race.

The Steeplechase is ⇒ exciting to watch.

HORSING AROUND

This horseback rider has a long way to go before he reaches the steeple. Help him wind his way through the park to get to the finish line.

NASHVILLE METROS

This fan is happy to have her shirt signed by one of the Metros.

Get the latest on the Metros' schedule and league standings on their web page, at www.nashville-metros.com.

More than 20,000 Nashville kids are registered soccer players on organized teams. When they're not playing, Nashvillians like to watch the soccer action of the city's exciting new professional team, the Metros. The Metros compete in soccer's A-League. Although newcomers, they finished second in the tough Central Division of the Western Conference in 1997.

The Metros' new stadium in Ezell Park, which will seat 15,000 spectators, will be completed no later than the summer of 1999. Meanwhile, the Metros play at their temporary home on Harding Place—the Columbia Soccer Stadium. The team hosts professional and amateur games, youth camps, youth clinics, and youth tournaments. Spectators are invited to arrive early and enjoy picnics, and participate in organized activities for families.

The Metros play teams from all over the United States and Canada, but their players come from even farther away: Mexico, Algeria, Surinam, Somalia, and Turkey are among the countries that Metros players call home.

WHAT'S THE DIFFERENCE?

These two pictures might look the same, but they are not. How many differences between the two scenes can you find? Hint: There are at least 15 differences.

OTHER SPORTS EVENTS IN NASHVILLE

Basketball excitement is provided by the **Commodores**, Vanderbilt University's team. The Commodores have won four championships in the very competitive Southeastern Conference (SEC) and play in Memorial Gym, the oldest gym in the SEC. One of the most famous former Commodores is Will Perdue. He used to play for the Chicago Bulls with Michael Jordan, and is now playing for the San Antonio Spurs.

Race car fans can go to **Nashville Speedway U.S.A.** where NASCAR stock car races run all summer on Saturday nights. When NASCAR is racing elsewhere, you can enjoy midget car races and races with other types of race cars.

⇑ **The starting booth at the Nashville Speedway**

START YOUR ENGINES

Without telling anyone what you're doing, ask for a word to fill in each blank. For example, "Give me an action word." When all the blanks are filled in, read the story out loud. One of the blanks has been filled in for you.

It was the day before the big race. Alex and Tim were __laugh__ing
                                                          action word

in the pit area inside the racetrack. Crews and drivers were working

on their cars. "_____!" said Alex. "There's _____. He's
                  exclamation   name 1

won _____ races this year." The boys ran over to look at his
       number

car. "This sure is a _____ car," Alex said. "Thanks,"
                      describing word

said _____. "I'm taking it on a test run around
       name 1

the track in a few minutes. How about a ride?" The boys

looked at each other in _____. Tim looked into the car.
                          emotion

"Sure," he said. "But where do we sit! There's only one seat." "No

problem," said _____. "You can ride on the _____."
                 name 1   things

WHERE TO PLAY

If you'd rather play a sport than watch one, check out the **Centennial Sportsplex**. This recreational center opened in 1990 and offers something for everyone. There are two pools, a skating rink, and tennis courts. Go for a swim in the **Tracy Caulkins Natatorium**, the pool named for the Nashville swimmer who won three Olympic gold medals.

Near Opryland you'll find three miniature-golf courses (two with 18 holes, and a 9-hole challenge course) at **Grand Old Golf**. When you've had enough golfing, go indoors to the game room. With 70 different arcade games, you're sure to find something you like. In warm weather, cool off and splash in the bumper boats.

Nashville's hot summers make **Wave Country** a popular spot. Slides lead into the giant pool, and the waves make you feel like you're in the ocean.

⬆ **The Centennial Sportsplex ice skating rink**

The world record for the 50-meter freestyle was set in the Tracy Caulkins Natatorium.

⬅ **The Tracy Caulkins Natatorium**

MY TRAVEL JOURNAL
—Good Sports—

I had fun when I visited: _____

My favorite sport is: _____

I like it because: _____

This is a picture of something I saw

6 MUSEUMS AND MORE

Do you want to learn more about country stars, Tennessee, and its people, art, science, toys, or life in the past? Pick any of these subjects, and you'll find a museum in Nashville to help you find out what you need to know. Don't worry that you might have to spend a beautiful day indoors—some of Nashville's museums are outdoors, so you can pick up knowledge and enjoy a nice day at the same time. Nashville's museums welcome kids, and you'll be sure to find a special activity in any area that interests you. Most museums have hands-on exhibits that you can touch or play with.

See the Kinetic Coaster at the Cumberland Science Museum.

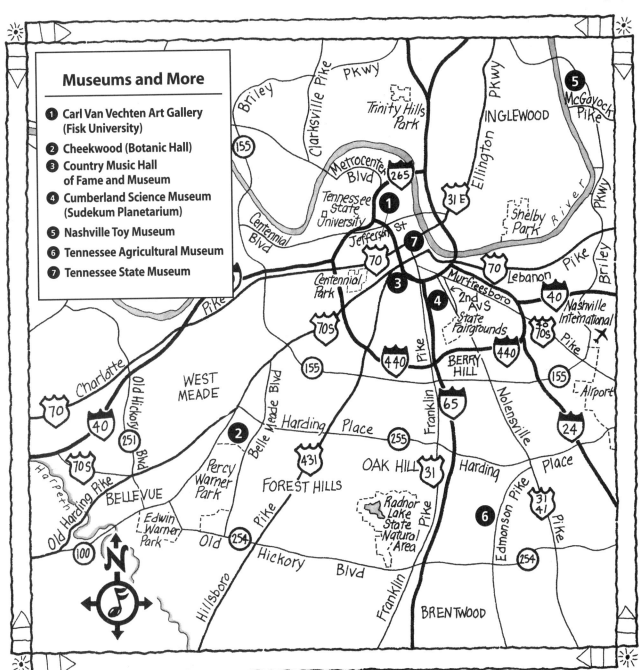

THE COUNTRY MUSIC HALL OF FAME AND MUSEUM

So many visitors come to the Country Music Hall of Fame and Museum that it has outgrown its small building on Music Row. So in 1998, they will move to a new and much bigger building directly across the street from the Nashville Arena. There will be changing exhibits on different country stars, and the permanent collection will show the history of country music.

At the current location of the hall of fame, you can try on sequined costumes, play a banjo or steel guitar, and imagine you're up on stage with Billy Ray Cyrus or Wynonna Judd. Pick up a booklet called *A Crash Course on Country* at the front desk and find the answers to the questions in the display cases throughout the Hall of Fame.

⬆ **Elvis Presley's talking Cadillac**

Have you ever heard of a talking car? Check out Elvis Presley's talking Cadillac in the Hall of Fame.

⬅ **Imagine you're a star at the Country Music Hall of Fame.**

HATS OFF TO COUNTRY MUSIC!

Some country music stars wear cowboy hats.
If you could design your own cowboy hat,
what would it look like? Decorate the hat above.

THE TENNESSEE STATE MUSEUM

Tennesseans are proud of their state's history. Be sure to visit the Tennessee State Museum to find out more about this great state.

The museum has exhibits that showcase objects from prehistoric times to modern times. The oldest of the more than 6,000 objects on display are fossils. The models of early Indian villages will show you what life was like thousands of years ago.

Can you imagine people wearing armor in Tennessee? Spanish explorers wore it, and you can see some at the museum. There are also objects that belonged to famous explorers David Crockett and Daniel Boone. You can see Civil War uniforms and weapons, a log cabin, a print shop, rooms set up with furniture from earlier centuries, quilts, paintings, and other objects from Tennessee's history. Some of the display cases have buttons you can push to hear a voice that will tell you about the exhibit.

You can actually touch the enormous tooth of a prehistoric mastodon at the state museum.

Firefighters used this horse-drawn fire engine in 1900.

CROSSWORD FUN

There are a lot of interesting facts to learn about Tennessee's state history. Solve this crossword by figuring out the clues or completing the sentences. If you need help, use the clue box.

Across

2. Another word for a small town.
5. Davey Crockett and Daniel Boone were _____ explorers.
7. You can see Civil War uniforms and _____ at the museum too.
8. Blankets made from many pieces of cloth.

Down

1. This was also called the war between the states.
3. You'll see a _____ cabin at the Tennessee Museum.
4. The opposite of stop.
6. These are the oldest things on exhibit at the museum.
7. Each settler had to dig one of these to get water.

Clue Box

well	bold
village	log
fossils	Civil War
quilts	weapons
go	

OSCAR L. FARRIS AGRICULTURAL MUSEUM

↑ **MacDonald Craig sings the blues at the museum.**

Can you imagine life without electricity? Before electricity was brought to the rural parts of the state, no lights, computers, dishwashers, or washing machines meant a lot more work for everyone, including the children. If you don't think you would have liked living in the time before electricity but would like to get an idea of what it was like back then, visit the Oscar L. Farris Agricultural Museum. The museum is in a barn that was built in 1927. Here you will see old farm equipment as well as everyday household goods on display.

The museum hosts a different program almost every month. Grind herbs with special tools called a mortar and pestle, wash clothes on a scrub board, or sweep a wooden floor with a corn broom. Learn how to make soap and weave baskets. You'll probably go home thankful that you lead a modern life!

THE GOOD OLD DAYS

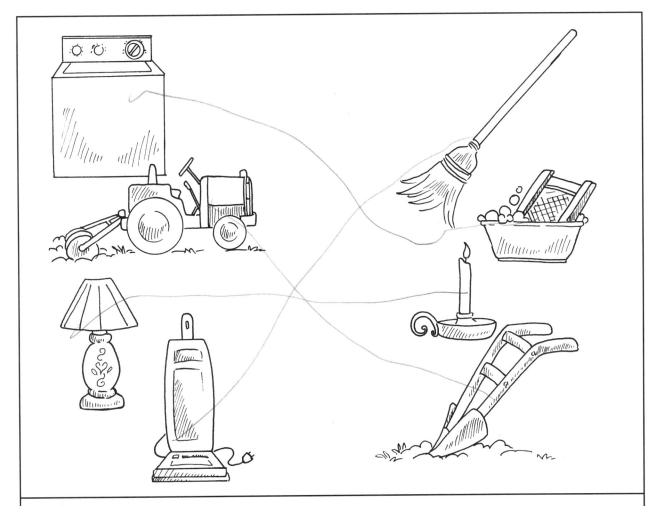

Farms did not have electricity in the eighteenth and nineteenth centuries, and many of the machines we use today did not exist. What do you think families used to do their chores? Draw a line from the modern machine to the old-fashioned object that did the same job.

CUMBERLAND SCIENCE MUSEUM

At the Cumberland Science Museum you can hear an explanation of animal behavior or see models of animals in their homes. The museum's **Sudekum Planetarium** gives tours of the galaxy several times a day.

But you don't have to just listen to people tell you about science. Try the Kinetic Coaster where you crank a handle to make a ball climb up to the top of a metal structure. Labels on the coaster explain the science of what is happening as the ball rockets back down to the starting point. You can also make beautiful music with a Chinese singing bowl, figure out why racetracks have tilted curves, and see for yourself if a ball goes faster down a steep hill or a shallow one (you may be surprised!).

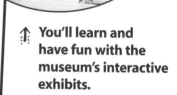

⬆ **You'll learn and have fun with the museum's interactive exhibits.**

Cumberland Science Museum ⇒

UNSCRAMBLE THE WORDS

NOMO _MORN_

MEOTC _____

ELNIA _____

ASTRS _____

SLETPAN _____

In this activity, unscramble each word, then draw a line
connecting the word to the correct picture.

Most of the toys in this museum were made before people had electricity in their homes, but some of the toys moved anyway. Can you figure out how they were set in motion?

THE NASHVILLE TOY MUSEUM

What kind of toys did your grandparents play with? Or their grandparents? Find out at the Nashville Toy Museum. The museum's owner, Edward H. Lannom III, started out building trains and cities for his toy soldiers when he was a boy. After a trip to the Smithsonian Institution in Washington, D.C., when he was in second grade, he decided he wanted a museum. He spent 19 years building the mountains and the city his model trains run through. Look for the model of Nashville's Union Station. When the staff isn't busy, you can ask them to get the trains running.

Aside from building trains and boats, Lannom has collected antique toys from all over the world. The oldest piece in the museum is a statue of a Scottish soldier from 1847. Imagine your great-grandparents as children playing with the model boats and cars, 100-year-old dolls with beautiful velvet outfits, wind-up circus acrobats, and teddy bears that are on display at the museum. They probably played with their toys a lot like you do now!

Your grandparents might have played with toys like these.

COLOR TO FIND THE ANSWER

**You might see one of these antique toys at the Nashville Toy Museum.
Use the following color code to find the hidden picture.
A=skin color, J=Gold, L=Blue, P=Black**

Each December, different garden clubs and other groups decorate trees for the holidays. The trees are displayed in Botanic Hall for Cheekwood's annual Trees of Christmas Festival.

CHEEKWOOD

Beautiful art in the middle of rolling hills and green fields—that's what makes Cheekwood special. Stop at **Botanic Hall** first. Many works of art seen in the great hall have nature themes, so you may see wildflower paintings or scenes of the outdoors. Imagine your own nature art hanging in the hall.

Cheekwood's new, contemporary art space opens in 1998 as part of the **Learning Center**. The old horse stables of the Cheek Estate will become an interactive learning center complete with computers for kids to use, art and nature activities, and a contemporary art gallery. Each horse stall will be made into a little art gallery for the work of local artists.

← Here is a preview of what the new Learning Center will look like.

DRAW YOUR OWN SCULPTURE

There is room for one more sculpture at Cheekwood and you get to design it! Draw your sculpture in the space above.

THE CARL VAN VECHTEN ART GALLERY

It used to be that art lovers had to go to big cities like New York and Chicago to see great art. A famous painter named Georgia O'Keeffe thought that was unfair, so in 1949, she gave 101 works of art to Fisk University so that people in the southeast could have the pleasure of seeing them. The gallery housing this artwork is the Carl Van Vechten Gallery at Fisk University.

Some of O'Keeffe's beautiful paintings of flowers and the desert are in the gallery. You can also find photographs by O'Keeffe's husband, Alfred Stieglitz. Stieglitz was an early collector of African art, and some of his favorite African sculptures are on display. There are also paintings by such famous artists as Paul Cézanne, Pablo Picasso, Diego Rivera, Pierre Auguste Renoir, and Henri de Toulouse-Lautrec.

⇡ **Carl Van Vechten Gallery at Fisk University**

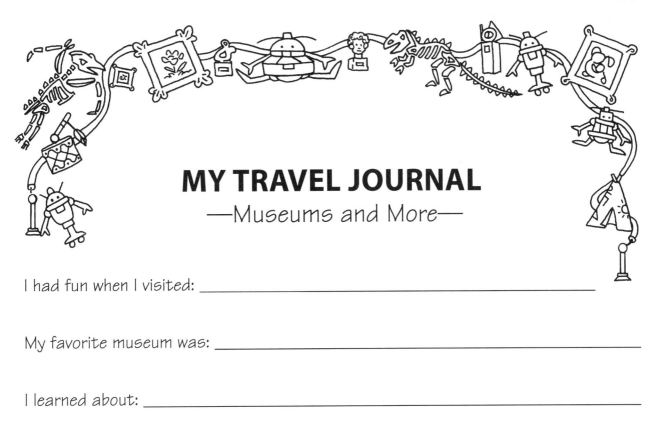

MY TRAVEL JOURNAL
—Museums and More—

I had fun when I visited: _____

My favorite museum was: _____

I learned about: _____

This is a picture of a painting or sculpture I saw

THAT'S ENTERTAINMENT

THE BIG ENTERTAINMENT ATTRACTION IN Nashville is country music. You can hear it performed, meet the stars, catch a glimpse of its history, and even make your own musical recording. The shops along Music Row sell every kind of country music souvenir you can imagine: posters, dolls, miniature guitars, hats, T-shirts, and more. People say that you might not be a country music fan when you first come to Nashville, but you probably will be one by the time you leave!

But don't forget to check out Nashville's other attractions, like an amusement park, miniature golf courses, theaters, and terrific shopping.

⇑ **Nashvillians enjoy the Nashville Mandolin Players.**

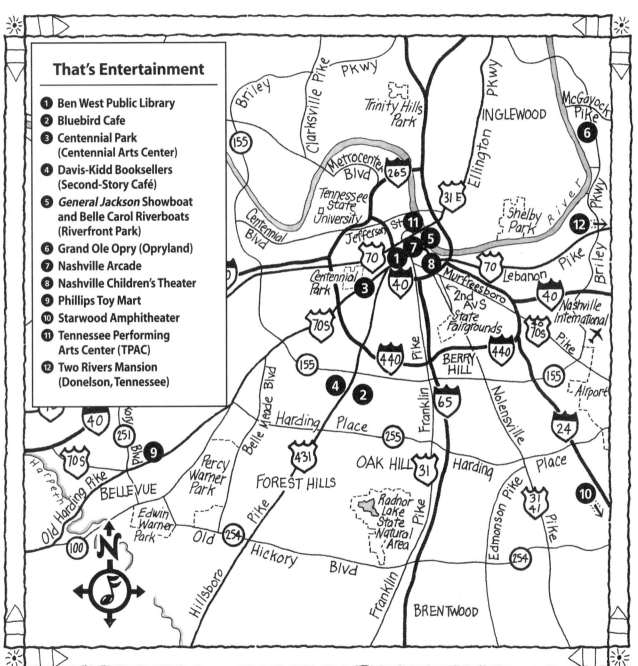

That's Entertainment

1. Ben West Public Library
2. Bluebird Cafe
3. Centennial Park
   (Centennial Arts Center)
4. Davis-Kidd Booksellers
   (Second-Story Café)
5. *General Jackson* Showboat
   and Belle Carol Riverboats
   (Riverfront Park)
6. Grand Ole Opry (Opryland)
7. Nashville Arcade
8. Nashville Children's Theater
9. Phillips Toy Mart
10. Starwood Amphitheater
11. Tennessee Performing
    Arts Center (TPAC)
12. Two Rivers Mansion
    (Donelson, Tennessee)

GRAND OLE OPRY

Opryland Hotel is the world's seventh largest hotel.

Ask your parents to call for reservations to the Grand Ole Opry.

Performances of the *Grand Ole Opry* started in 1925, making it the world's longest-running radio show. The shows are so popular that you should reserve your tickets well in advance of a visit, especially in the summer. The schedules aren't set until a few days before each performance, so you have to trust your luck that you'll see your favorite star. No matter who's performing, you're guaranteed a treat.

This huge theater was constructed in 1974 when the Ryman Auditorium became too small to hold all the crowds that enjoyed going to the Opry. The theater seats 4,424 people. Matinees and evening shows are usually sold out, especially in the summer. Stars such as Garth Brooks and Reba McEntire perform to cheering crowds.

Be sure to stop in at the Opryland Hotel and Conference Center. Take a ride on a flatboat down the Delta River, a 4 1/2-acre river lined with shops and even a 110-foot-wide waterfall!

MIXED-UP PICTURE STORY

To find out what is happening at the Grand Ole Opry, put the scenes in the correct order by filling in the number box in the bottom corner of each picture.

THE *GENERAL JACKSON* SHOWBOAT AND THE BELLE CAROL RIVERBOATS

You don't have to stay on dry land to enjoy great music in Nashville. Climb aboard the *General Jackson* for an evening of food and music. The entertainment schedule changes often, but whatever the show, it always pleases a music-loving crowd. Sometimes it's a Broadway-style show, sometimes it's a rock band, and sometimes it's a country singer. The boat is 300 feet long, so there are plenty of places to explore between music shows. Dinner is served on most cruises. If you're a night owl, you can take a midnight cruise during Fan Fair, a week-long country music celebration held each June.

The Belle Carol operates two different paddle wheelers that run from March through December. You can eat on board and, besides listening to musical entertainment, you can get a history lesson about Nashville as you go down the river.

⬆ **The *General Jackson* looks beautiful at night.**

The *General Jackson* is the largest showboat in the world.

WHAT'S WRONG WITH THIS PICTURE?

It's a strange day on the riverboat cruise and lots of
things are out of place. Circle 12 things you think are wrong
with this picture and then color in the scene.

BLUEBIRD CAFE

Maybe you'll see a famous singer at the Bluebird Cafe.

"I saw Garth Brooks perform at the Bluebird before he was famous!" Do you wish you could say that about a star? At the Bluebird Cafe, you just might see tomorrow's great country stars before anyone has ever heard of them. Garth Brooks, Kathy Mattea, Pam Tillis, and Vince Gill all played at the Bluebird and went on to become legends of country music. Well-known stars still come to the Bluebird to try out new music before playing it for a larger audience. So don't be surprised if one of them turns up without warning.

The early show is at 6:45 p.m., and you can have dinner while enjoying the music. There's no kids' menu, but with chicken fingers, pizza, and tortellini to choose from, almost everyone will find something they like.

Don't just look for country music stars on the stage at the Bluebird, check out the audience. Lots of stars come here to listen to music, too!

THE PLACE TO BE

Hidden in this word search are things you might see or do at the Bluebird Cafe. Search for the words vertically, horizontally, and diagonally. Can you find all 10 words? The first word has been found for you.

Word Box

stars	sing	clap
guitar	stage	drums
dance	music	
microphone	food	

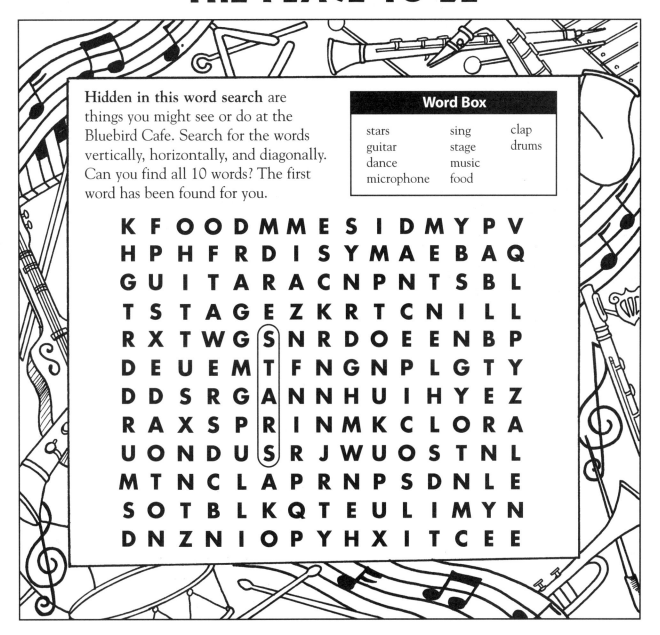

```
K F O O D M M E S I D M Y P V
H P H F R D I S Y M A E B A Q
G U I T A R A C N P N T S B L
T S T A G E Z K R T C N I L L
R X T W G S N R D O E E N B P
D E U E M T F N G N P L G T Y
D D S R G A N N H U I H Y E Z
R A X S P R I N M K C L O R A
U O N D U S R J W U O S T N L
M T N C L A P R N P S D N L E
S O T B L K Q T E U L I M Y N
D N Z N I O P Y H X I T C E E
```

AT THE LIBRARY

Even in the library, you don't have to open a book to find a good story. You can see one performed by the Paint the Town Players. They perform with puppets controlled by strings or marionettes, and they are based at Nashville's downtown **Ben West Public Library**. The beautiful marionettes the players use were handmade by Tom Tichenor, who also wrote a lot of the plays that are performed on the library's large stage. Both fairy tales and original stories can be seen every week. The library's **Prime Time Puppets** perform more often. They tell stories most Wednesday mornings and sometimes on the weekends, too.

All branches of the Nashville library have story hours. At the southeast branch you can even hear a story in Spanish!

⇑ **Tom Tichenor marionettes at the library**

⇐ **Puppet Playhouse at the Ben West Public Library**

HIDE & SEEK

Can you find all of the hidden objects in this picture of the library?
Hint: There are at least 14 objects.

PERFORMING ARTS

The Nashville Children's Theater is the country's third oldest professional children's theater company.

Be sure your parents come with you to a performance of the **Nashville Children's Theater**—you'll both have a great time. Their mission is "creating meaningful art for young audiences," and to reach this goal they produce their own original plays as well as plays written by others. Some involve audience participation, so polish up on your acting skills before you go!

The **Tennessee Performing Arts Center** (locally known as TPAC, pronounced TEE-pack) is home to three separate theaters, each one named for a United States president from Tennessee. In addition, the **Nashville Ballet**, the **Nashville Symphony**, and the **Nashville Opera** all perform at TPAC.

⇐ Imagine yourself playing in the Nashville Symphony.

THE LONELY BALLERINA

One of the ballerinas in the show does not have a partner. Draw a line connecting the matching ballerinas to find the one without a partner.

↥ **Davis-Kidd Booksellers**

The design of the Nashville Arcade was inspired by the Galleria, a nineteenth-century shopping mall in Milan, Italy.

SHOPPING

Ready for some shopping? Start out at **Phillips Toy Mart**. Founded in 1946, it's crammed full of every kind of toy you can imagine. The store specializes in collectibles, especially electric trains, dolls, and dollhouse accessories. But you'll also find puzzles, sports equipment, board games, china figurines, art supplies, and everything else you can think of.

The block-long **Nashville Arcade**, which connects Fourth and Fifth Avenues, was built in 1903. Here you will find many different stores and restaurants, including The Peanut Shop, where you can buy a bag of fresh-roasted peanuts to munch while you sightsee.

The children's collection at **Davis-Kidd Booksellers** is full of every kind of kids' book you can imagine. If all this book browsing leaves you feeling hungry, stop at the **Second-Story Café** in the bookstore for lunch and one of their fabulous desserts. Storytellers, singers, and other performers entertain on weekends in the Kidd's Corner series.

WHAT'S IN COMMON?

Each bag of popcorn has something in common with the
two others in the same row. For example, the bags in the middle row all
have stripes on them. Draw lines through each row and describe what
the bags in that row have in common. Don't forget diagonals!

OUTDOOR ENTERTAINMENT

Take advantage of Nashville's mild weather and get some of your entertainment outdoors.

Centennial Park has great outdoor festivals for kids. You can hear storytellers or see theater and magic shows. On Friday nights in May, listen to music at the Stories Under the Stars series in the **Centennial Arts Center**. On Tuesday mornings in July, you can hear the Tales from Two Rivers series at **Two Rivers Mansion** in nearby Donelson, Tennessee. On Tuesday evenings during June and July, free movies are shown at the Centennial Park band shell. The park also sponsors special events throughout the summer at community centers. And be sure to check out the Shakespeare festival, where plays are performed outdoors at the band shell, and the Nashville Symphony outdoor performances. Both festivals are free.

If you like music—country, rock, alternative, or classical—you'll love the **Starwood Amphitheater** where you and up to 17,000 other people can picnic while listening to some of the country's biggest stars.

⬆ **Outdoor concerts are great fun.**

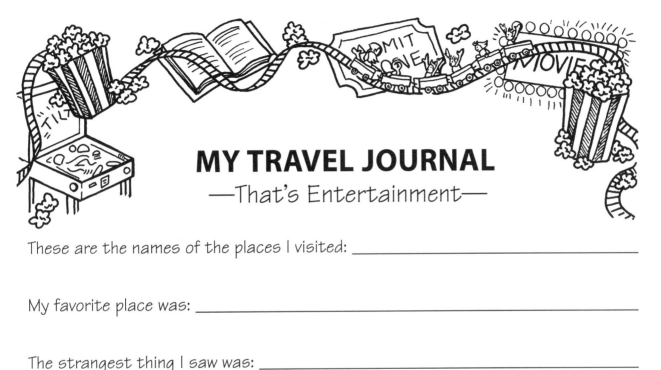

MY TRAVEL JOURNAL
—That's Entertainment—

These are the names of the places I visited: _____

My favorite place was: _____

The strangest thing I saw was: _____

This is a picture of something I saw

8 LET'S EAT

Be prepared to loosen your belt after a meal in Nashville. The favorite kind of restaurant here is the "meat-and-three" where you get to choose one meat and three vegetables or side dishes from a list of such home-cooked delights as macaroni and cheese, fried okra, applesauce, succotash, green beans, French fries, butter beans, and fried green tomatoes. Sometimes it's hard to stop at just three!

It's hard to imagine getting tired of "down-home" cooking, but if you do, Nashville's restaurants offer just about every other type of food you could want. If you like spicy food, Nashville has restaurants that serve Indian, Thai, and Mexican food. There are also lots of restaurants that serve food from Asian countries such as Korea, China, and Japan. From American home cooking to foreign delights from far-away countries, Nashville's restaurants will keep you filled with good food.

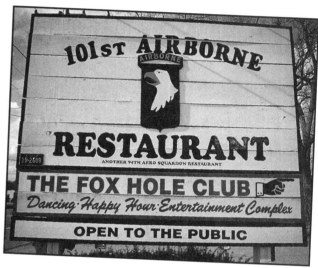

⬆ **Look for the airplane out in front of the 101st Airborne restaurant.**

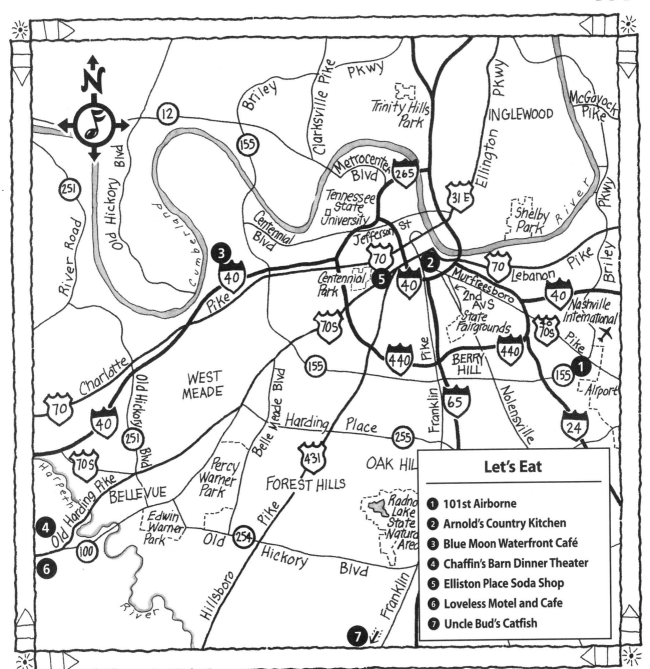

Let's Eat

1. 101st Airborne
2. Arnold's Country Kitchen
3. Blue Moon Waterfront Café
4. Chaffin's Barn Dinner Theater
5. Elliston Place Soda Shop
6. Loveless Motel and Cafe
7. Uncle Bud's Catfish

ARNOLD'S COUNTRY KITCHEN

⇑ **The crew at Arnold's Country Kitchen**

Look for country music stars, construction workers, and shoppers who have just come out of the antique store next door. Everybody comes to Arnold's!

Be sure to leave plenty of time—and room in your stomach—if you want to eat at Arnold's. It's a popular lunch spot for people who enjoy good old-fashioned country cooking. You might have to wait in line for a while to get served cafeteria-style. There's no menu at Arnold's, just a constantly changing variety of food from which to choose.

So when you get close to the food and see what they have that day, you'll have to make up your mind on the spot. This can be hard when you're faced with such great dishes as fried chicken, turkey and dressing, homestyle meatloaf, and pork chops. There are baked apples, macaroni and cheese, mashed potatoes and gravy, all kinds of beans—green beans, lima beans, white beans—coleslaw, and fresh vegetables in season. You can always count on a large assortment of pies and cobbler for dessert.

SO MANY CHOICES!

GREEN BEANS   CHICKEN   MACARONI   MASHED POTATOES   GRAVY

Cafeteria-style restaurants like Arnold's offer so many choices. What would you order if you went to a restaurant that features country cooking? Draw the meal you would choose on this plate. Don't forget your vegetables!

ELLISTON PLACE SODA SHOP

Take a step back in time at the Elliston Place Soda Shop. This old-fashioned diner has been in operation since 1939 and it hasn't changed much since then. The booths and tables are set close together, and the cheerful waitresses are always rushing around the restaurant to deliver orders. It's hard to decide what to order, but try the cheeseburger and fries, or the crispy fried chicken.

If you look up on the wall behind the counter, you'll see where the soda shop gets its name. You'll see pictures of sodas, sundaes, floats—anything you can imagine making with ice cream. The chocolate milkshakes at Elliston Place are the best in town.

About the only thing that has been modernized at the soda shop is the selection of tunes on the 1950s-style jukebox. Choose your favorite 1990s tune to listen to while you eat.

⇡ **This soda shop has been serving ice-cream sundaes since 1939.**

SODA POP AND ROCK

You'll have "scoops" of fun at Elliston Place Soda Shop. Solve this crossword by figuring out the clues or completing the sentences. If you need help, use the clue box.

Across

1. Elliston Place is a _____ _____.
4. What you'd call a small restaurant.
6. North, South, West, or _____.
8. You can sit in a booth or at one of these at the diner.
9. Your waitress will _____ your meal to you.

Down

1. Ice-cream desserts with toppings are called these.
2. A polite way to ask for something.
3. Opposite of worst.
5. Visiting the Elliston Place Soda Shop is like stepping back in _____.
7. What you do when you wiggle, or a drink made with milk and ice cream.

Clue Box

please	table	soda shop
east	best	serve
shake	diner	
sundaes	time	

LOVELESS MOTEL AND CAFE

There's no longer a motel at the Loveless Motel and Cafe, but the restaurant is busier than ever. Here you will find the best of old-fashioned country cooking. This is a great breakfast spot, and their homemade preserves and biscuits top everyone's list of favorites. You can buy preserves to take home as you leave. Country ham is served with any style of eggs you can think of. Homemade sausage is also available. Stick around for lunch or dinner and you'll find home-style fried chicken, pork chops, and other specialties of the southeast.

The Loveless Motel is popular with visitors, but also with people from Nashville and the farms nearby. You might catch a glimpse of a country music star digging into a plate of fried eggs and grits, or a farmer enjoying a breakfast out with his family.

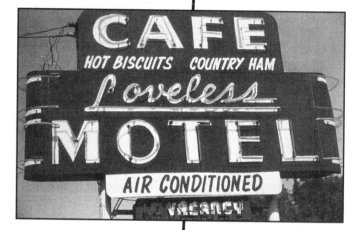

⇑ **Old-fashioned country cooking hits the spot at the Loveless Motel and Cafe.**

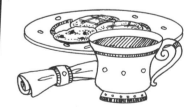

WHAT'S THE DIFFERENCE?

These two scenes of the Loveless Motel and Cafe might look the same, but they are not. How many differences between the two scenes can you find? Hint: There are at least 15 differences.

UNCLE BUD'S CATFISH

Nashville is a long way from the ocean, but that doesn't stop Nashvillians from eating fish. The lakes and streams near Nashville attract many fishermen trying to catch bluegill, bass, and especially catfish. Catfish live on the bottoms of the rivers and can grow several feet long, although most of them are caught when they are only a foot or so in length. Some people don't like the taste of these fish because they think the fish taste muddy. Catfish are now being raised on "catfish ranches" where the fish are fed a special diet to make their taste less strong.

You can get both wild or farm-raised catfish at one of Uncle Bud's several locations in Nashville. To make it a truly southern meal, you can order side dishes such as cole slaw and hush puppies, which are tasty, bite-sized pieces of fried cornmeal and seasonings.

Hush puppies were originally bits of cornmeal that fishermen removed from the frying pan, then tossed to their dogs saying, "Hush, puppy!"

HUSH PUPPY!

This puppy can smell the catfish cooking at Uncle Bud's Catfish and wants to get there. Can you help him?

NEAT SCENERY WHILE YOU EAT

The **101st Airborne** is a restaurant that's easy to spot—just look for the huge airplane out front. The restaurant is decorated in a World War II theme and you can also see tanks and other military machines. While you wait for your meal, put on the headphones you find at every table to listen to the talk between the air traffic controllers and the pilots of the planes taking off at the nearby Nashville International Airport.

If you'd rather hear the sound of water while you dine, try the **Blue Moon Waterfront Café.** You can get a closeup look at the Cumberland River when you eat at a table sitting right on the dock at the Rock Harbor Marina. Be sure to try the catfish nuggets on the kids' menu.

To eat and see a musical or comedy performed, **Chaffin's Barn Dinner Theater** is the place for you. Choose your own meal from an all-you-can-eat buffet, and just as you're finishing up, a stage is lowered from the ceiling and a play begins.

The Blue Moon Café has its own herb garden to flavor the fish and other food.

Listen to air traffic controllers through the headphones at your table.

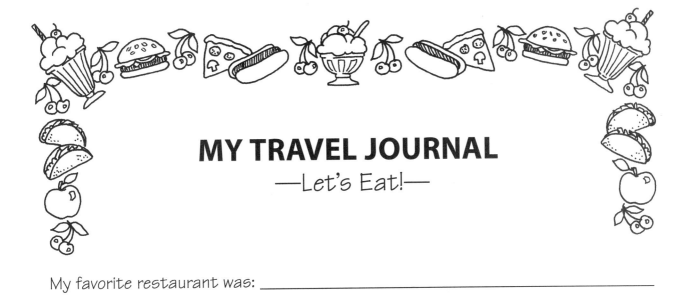

MY TRAVEL JOURNAL
—Let's Eat!—

My favorite restaurant was: _____

The most unusual food I ate was: _____

My least favorite food was: _____

This is a picture of one restaurant I visited

CALENDAR OF NASHVILLE EVENTS

Celebrate Nashville and Nashvillians year-round at different festivals, shows, and exhibits. Local people attend all these fairs, and you can, too. Just call ahead for exact dates of the attractions mentioned.

January
Nashville Boat and Sport Show
Convention Center, Nashville, (615) 742-7000. For five days

⚑ **Waterskiing on Percy Priest Lake**

around the second weekend in January, the Nashville Convention Center hosts a boat and sport show with different attractions for young people every year, such as a shark tank, fishing demonstration, and a kids' casting contest.

February
Americana Sampler Craft, Folk Art, and Antique Fair
State Fairgrounds, Nashville, (615) 227-2080. Said to be the largest craft fair in the country, the Americana Sampler also has craft demonstrations, music, and dancing. It is scheduled for the first weekend in February each year and is also held in April, August, and November.

Black History Month Celebration
Nashville State Technical Institute, Nashville, (615) 353-3267. All through the month of February, the library has a display of posters and information on African Americans. Festivities

include African dance and music, an outdoor display with arts and crafts, speakers, a talent show, and a soul food unity luncheon.

Bobby Jones Gospel Explosion
Tennessee Performing Arts Center, Nashville, (615) 665-1009. Famed gospel artist Bobby Jones wants people to know that gospel isn't just singing, it's a way of life. To show this, not only singers, but lecturers, drummers, mimes, ventriloquists, and dancers all perform at this three-day "explosion," the largest

⬆ **He's having fun at the library.**

gathering of gospel artists in the world. Another explosion is held each July.

March
Festival of Flight
Cumberland Museum, Nashville, (615) 862-5160. You can make and fly kites, participate in a paper airplane contest, and watch some fantastic creations soar through the air at this springtime festival.

Easter Art Hop
Cheekwood, Nashville, (615) 356-8000. This family discovery day combines both of Cheekwood's specialties—art and nature. Visitors make sidewalk art drawings and sculpture. The Nashville Ballet and Nashville Repertory Theater put on performances. On the nature side, visitors plant seeds, learn about plants, and often receive a plant to take home.

April
Zoofest
Nashville Zoo, Nashville, (615) 370-3333. Participate in crafts, see animals closeup, and play at the Jungle Gym.

Al Menah Temple Shrine Circus
Municipal Auditorium, Nashville, (615) 259-6217. This circus benefits the Shrine's Children's Hospital.

May
Historic Rural Life Festival
Oscar L. Farris Agricultural Museum, Nashville, (615) 360-0197. Learn how people lived the eighteenth and nineteenth centuries. Try your hand at basket weaving, soap making, and other activities.

Tennessee Crafts Fair
Centennial Park, Nashville, (615) 665-0502. This open-air crafts fair features demonstrations and many children's activities.

Iroquois Steeplechase

Percy Warner Park, Nashville, (615) 322-7450. Celebrate one of horse racing's major events and benefit the Vanderbilt's Children's Hospital.

Tennessee Renaissance Festival

Castle Gwynn, Triune, (615) 395-7050. Jousts, jugglers, elephant rides, games, and food—all take place at one man's personal castle.

Days on the Farm

Sam Davis Home, Smyrna, (615) 459-2341. Living history activities such as open-fire cooking, spinning, weaving, and blacksmithing will introduce you to life on a prosperous nineteenth-century farm.

Opryland Gospel Jubilee

Opryland Hotel, 2800 Opryland Drive, Nashville, (615) 889-1000. Hear gospel music performed over Memorial Day Weekend.

June

Ear Foundation Balloon Classic

Edwin Warner Park, Nashville, (615) 329-7807. See brightly-colored hot air balloons take to the air in this annual event. Balloon rides are available. This event benefits the Ear Foundation.

American Artisan Festival

Centennial Park, Nashville, (615) 298-4691. This outdoor festival attracts 150 craftspeople from 35 states. There is a

children's art booth with activities. Musicians play all day on the weekend.

International Country Music Fan Fair

Tennessee State Fairgrounds, Nashville, (615) 889-7503. Tickets go on sale on January 1 and usually sell out within a month, so plan early. The fair lasts a week, and about 25,000 people attend to meet their favorite country stars, go to a bluegrass concert, or see the Grand Masters Fiddling Championship.

Summer Lights in Music City

Downtown Nashville, (615) 259-0900. Outdoor music and theater highlight this festival. There is a children's arts arcade.

The Nashville skyline

July
Independence Day Celebration
Riverfront Park, Nashville, (615) 862-8400. Not only a great fireworks show, but music, dance, and other entertainment help make the Fourth of July special in Nashville.

Little Spoleto
Cheekwood, Nashville, (615) 356-8000. Nashville's version of the Spoleto Arts Festival is a one-day activity day in July or August. You can see performances by the Nashville

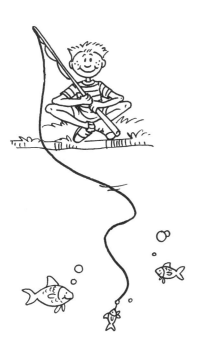

Ballet, the Nashville Repertory Theater, and African drums. There are art activities and refreshments.

August
Nashville Shakespeare Festival
Centennial Park, Nashville, (615) 862-8400. Enjoy Shakespeare under the stars on August weekends.

Annual Tennessee Walking Horse Celebration
Celebration Grounds, Shelbyville, (615) 684-5915. These high-stepping horses compete in front of 30,000 people each summer. One day of the festival is devoted to young riders.

September
Annual African Street Festival
Tennessee State University, Nashville, (615) 299-0412. Music, poetry, storytelling, and food celebrate African and African American life. The children's pavilion has different activities each year. Co-sponsored by the African American Cultural Alliance.

⇡ **Barbara the elephant bathing at the Elephant Sanctuary.**

Italian Street Fair
Maryland Farms, Brentwood, (615) 329-3033. Arts and crafts booths, Italian American food, and music come together for a celebration that benefits the Nashville Symphony.

Civil War Encampment
Traveller's Rest Historic House Museum, Nashville, (615) 832-8197. People dressed in authentic Civil War uniforms reenact an encampment. A children's

section has various activities. There are lectures on the Civil War and Nashville's part in it.

Tennessee State Fair

State Fairgrounds, Nashville, (615) 862-8993 or 862-8980. This old-fashioned fair has a lively midway with many games, rides, and booths. Be sure to stop in the livestock areas and admire the mules, pigs, cows, sheep, rabbits, chickens, and other animals.

October

Grand Ole Opry Birthday

Opryland, Nashville, (615) 889-6611. In this three-day celebration you can meet stars and get their autographs. Music and dance are performed.

Germantown Oktoberfest

1227 Seventh Avenue North, Nashville, (615) 256-2729. Nashvillians of German descent celebrate this traditional holiday with German food, music, dancing, arts and crafts booths, and clowns.

Music and Molasses Festival

Oscar L. Farris Agricultural Museum, Nashville, (615) 360-0197. Participate in traditional arts and other activities.

Native American Indian Association Pow Wow

Location varies, Nashville, (615) 726-0806. Native Americans from all over the United States and Canada gather for a three-day festival of food, dancing, and music.

Storytelling Festival

The Hermitage, Hermitage, (615) 889-2941. Three days of storytelling and festivities at the home of United States President Andrew Jackson.

⇡ **The Nashville Parthenon at Centennial Park**

Southern Festival of Books
Legislative Plaza, Nashville, (615) 320-7001. Book sales, readings, children's activities, storytelling, autographs, and lectures for all book lovers.

November
Christmas at Belle Meade Plantation
Nashville, (615) 356-0501. Celebrate a traditional nineteenth-century Christmas at this gracious mansion, once the home of one of the world's most important thoroughbred horse farms.

Longhorn World Championship Rodeo
Nashville, (615) 876-1016 or 357-6336. This old-fashioned rodeo is complete with calf roping, bronco busting, and colorful clowns.

December
Trees of Christmas
Cheekwood, Nashville, (615) 352-5310. Different garden clubs in Middle Tennessee decorate trees, all with a single theme for the year. Crafts are on sale.

RESOURCE GUIDE:
WHEN, WHAT, AND WHERE

Nashvillians are very friendly people. In fact, Nashville was chosen as the seventh friendliest city in the country in 1996. Be courteous in return and remember that although children are welcome at all the attractions in this resource guide, you will be expected to behave with consideration toward everyone.

Dates, times, and locations of attractions listed often change from year to year, so be sure to call ahead to check information, as well as for admission prices. Most parks are open from sunrise to sunset. For information on city parks, call (615) 862-8400.

If You Get Lost

Stay safe while visiting Music City. Here are some tips to keep you and your adult companions together:

Wear a hat. Choose a bright-colored baseball cap and wear it whenever you might be in a crowd.

Be prepared. Agree ahead of time on a safe place to meet if you get separated.

"I see you, you see me—that's the way it has to be." If you can see the adults you're with, that means they can see you, too. If you lose sight of them, stay put and look around. If you can't see them, go to your agreed-on location.

Be wary of strangers. Most people like children and want to help them, but that's not always

⇪ **The Commodores play at Vanderbilt University.**

the case. Decide on a password ahead of time so if you get lost you'll only go with a stranger that your adult companions trust enough to tell the password to.

Money. Be sure to carry enough money to make a phone call and to buy a snack if you have a long wait before you're picked up.

Take notes. Write down the name and phone number of your hotel, people you're staying with,

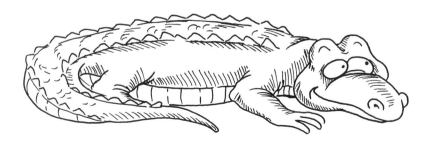

or tour group. Carry this paper with you at all times.

Don't panic if you get separated from your group or your parents. If you're in a park, go to a trail or road if you can see one and stay in one spot until people come by. If you can't see a road or trail, stay put and listen for searchers. They'll eventually show up.

Important Numbers

Injury, accident, or emergency, 911
Nashville Police (non-emergency), (615) 862-8600
Poison Control, (615) 936-2034
Tennessee State Safety Department, (615) 741-3954

Transportation

Grand Ole Opry Tours, (615) 889-9490

Gray Line Country and Western Tours, (615) 883-0235
Gray Line Sightseeing Tours, (615) 883-5555
Johnny Walker Tours, (615) 834-8585
Metropolitan Nashville Airport Authority, (615) 275-2675
Nashville Trolley Company, (615) 351-RIDE

Other Services

Fall Color Hotline, (615) 741-9026
Tennessee State Parks Information Hotline, (800) 421-6683.
Tourist Information, 161 Fourth Avenue North, (615) 259-4700. Open 8:00 a.m.–5:00 p.m. Operated by the Chamber of Commerce.
Tourist Information Center, Nashville Arena; (615) 259-4747.

Where They Are and When They're Open

101st Airborne, 1360 Murfreesboro Pike, Nashville, TN 37217; (615) 361-4212. Open Monday through Thursday, 11:00 a.m.–10:00 p.m.; Friday and Saturday, 11:00 a.m.–11:00 p.m.; Sunday, 10:00

⇧ **See a Picasso at the Tennessee State Museum.**

a.m.–2:00 p.m. and 4:00 p.m.–11:00 p.m.

Americana Craft Sampler Craft Art and Antique Fair, State Fairgrounds; (615) 228-5370. Call ahead for dates.

Arnold's Country Kitchen, 605 8th Avenue South, Nashville, TN 37203; (615) 256-4455. Open Monday through Friday, 6:00 a.m.–2:30 p.m.

Belle Meade Mansion, 5025 Harding Road, Nashville, TN 37205; (615) 269-9537.

Belmont Mansion, 1900 Belmont Boulevard, Nashville, TN 37212, (615) 460-5459. Open Tuesday through Saturday 10:00 am.–4:00 p.m.. In June, July, and August open Monday through Saturday, 10:00 a.m.–4:00 p.m.; Sunday, 2:00 p.m.–5:00 p.m. Admission: $6 for adults, $2 for children ages 6 to 12.

Bicentennial Mall, foot of Legislative Hill, Nashville, TN. Open daily.

Blue Moon Waterfront Café, 525 Basswood Avenue, Nashville, TN 37209; (615) 352-5892. Open Monday through Friday, 5:00 p.m.–10:00 p.m.;

⇑ **Bicentennial Mall**

Saturday, 5:00 p.m.–11:00 p.m.; Sunday, 12:00 p.m.–10:00 p.m.

Bluebird Cafe, 4104 Hillsboro Pike, Nashville, TN 37215; (615) 383-1461. Open Monday through Saturday, 5:30 p.m.–1:00 a.m.; Sunday, 6:00 a.m.–12:00 a.m.

Carl Van Vechten Art Gallery, Fisk University, 1000 17th Avenue North, Nashville, TN 37208; (615) 329-8720. Open Tuesday through Friday, 10:00 a.m.–5:00 p.m.; Saturday and Sunday, 1:00 p.m.–4:00 p.m.

Centennial Parks special programs, (615) 862-8424. Call for details on the Stories Under the Stars and Tales from Two Rivers series.

Centennial Sportsplex, 222 20th Avenue North, Nashville, TN 37203; (615) 862-8480. Hours vary, so call ahead. Fees for swimming and ice skating $4 for ages 12 and under, $5 for ages 13 and up. Tennis Center, (615) 862-8490. Hours vary, so call ahead.

Chaffin's Barn Dinner Theater, 8204 Highway 100, Nashville, TN 37221; (615) 646-9977.

Open Tuesday through Saturday, 6:00 p.m.–7:30 p.m. for dinner. Shows start at 8:00 p.m.

Cheatham Wildlife Management Area, Cheatham County, TN; (615) 792-4510. Hours vary, so call ahead.

Cheekwood, 1200 Forrest Park Drive, Nashville, TN 37205; (615) 356-8000 or 352-8632. Open Monday through Saturday, 9:00 a.m.–5:00 p.m.; Sunday 11:00 a.m.–5:00 p.m. (Museum of Art closed until mid-1999.)

Columbia Soccer Stadium, 5135 Harding Place, Nashville, TN 37211.

Country Music Hall of Fame and Museum, 4 Music Square East, Nashville, TN 37203; (615) 255-5333. Open daily 9:00 a.m.–5:00 p.m.

Cumberland Science Museum, 800 Fort Negley Boulevard, Nashville, TN 37203; (615) 862-5160. Open Tuesday through Saturday, 9:30 a.m.–5:00 p.m.; Sunday 12:30 p.m.–5:30 p.m.

Disability Information Office, Howard Office Building, 25 Middleton Street, Nashville, TN 37210; (615) 862-6492.

Downtown Presbyterian Church, 154 Fifth Avenue North, Nashville, TN 37219; (615) 254-7584. Hours vary, so call ahead.

 Fort Nashborough

The Elephant Sanctuary, P.O. Box 393, Hohenwald, TN 38462; (800) 98-TRUNK. Call ahead for hours and information on visiting.

Elliston Place Soda Shop, 2111 Elliston Place, Nashville, TN 37203; (615) 327-1090. Open Monday through Saturday, 6:00 a.m.–8:00 p.m.

Fannie Mae Dees Park (Dragon Park), 2400 Blakemore Avenue between 24th and 26th Avenue, Nashville, TN.

Fort Nashborough, 170 First Avenue, 170 First Avenue North, Nashville, TN 37201; (615) 255-8192. Open during daylight hours.

Grand Old Golf, 2444 Music Valley Drive, Nashville, TN 37214; (615) 871-4701. Hours vary, call ahead. Group rates available.

Grand Ole Opry, 2804 Opryland Drive, Nashville, TN 37214; (615) 889-6600. Hours vary, so call ahead.

The Hermitage, 4580 Rachel's Lane, Hermitage, TN 37076-1344; (615) 889-2941. Open daily, 9:00 a.m.–5:00 p.m.

Loveless Motel and Cafe, 8400 Highway 100, Nashville, TN; (615) 646-9700. Open Monday through Friday, 8:00 a.m.–2:00 p.m. and 5:00 p.m.–9:00 p.m.

Metropolitan Board of Parks and Recreation, (615) 862-8400.

Nashville Area Chamber of Commerce, 161 Fourth Avenue North, Nashville, TN 37219; (615) 259-4755.

Nashville Arena, 501 Broadway, Nashville, TN 37203; (615) 770-2000.

Nashville Children's Theater, 724 Second Avenue South, Nashville, TN 37210; (615) 254-7045 or (615) 254-9103.

Nashville Convention Center, 601 Commerce Street, Nashville, TN 37203; (615) 742-2000.

Nashville Kats, Nashville Area, 501 Broadway, Nashville, TN 37203; (615) 254-5287. Season runs end of April through end of July.

Nashville Metros Professional Soccer Club, 2214 Metro Center Boulevard, Suite 110, Nashville, TN, 37228; (615) 771-8200. Season runs May through August. Ticket prices vary; call ahead.

Nashville Municipal Auditorium, 417 Fourth Avenue North, Nashville, TN, 37219; (615) 862-6390.

Nashville Sounds Baseball, Greer Stadium, 534 Chestnut Avenue, Nashville, TN 37203; (615) 242-4371. Season runs April through early September.

⇑ **Canoe on the Harpeth River.**

Nashville Speedway U.S.A., 625 Smith Avenue, P.O. Box 40307, Nashville, TN 37204; (615) 726-1818. Some events have reserved seats only.

Narrows of the Harpeth State Park, Route 2, Kingston Springs, TN 37082.

Nashville Toy Museum, 2613 McGavock Pike, Nashville, TN 37214; (615) 883-8870. Hours vary, so call ahead.

Nashville Zoo, 1710 Ridge Circle, Joelton, TN 37080; (615) 370-3333. Open every day except January 1 and December 25, 10:00 a.m.–5 p.m.

Opryland Hotel and Conference Center, 2800 Opryland Drive, Nashville, TN 37214; (615) 889-1000

Oscar L. Farris Agricultural Museum, Tennessee Dept. of Agriculture, Ellington Agricultural Center, Nashville, TN 37204; (615) 837-5197.

Phillips Toy Mart, 5207 Harding Road, Nashville, TN 37205; (615) 352-5363. Open

Monday through Saturday, 9:00 a.m.–5:00 p.m.

Public Library of Nashville and Davidson County, Ben West Branch (main library), 225 Polk Avenue at Union Street, Nashville, TN 37203; 862-5800.

Radnor Lake State Natural Area, 1160 Otter Creek Road, Nashville, TN 37220; (615) 373-3467.

Ryman Auditorium, 116 Fifth Avenue North, Nashville, TN 37219; (615) 254-1445.

Sam Davis Home, 1399 Sam Davis Road, Smyrna, TN 37167;

(615) 459-2341. September to May, hours are Monday through Saturday, 10:00 a.m.–4:00 p.m.; Sunday 1:00 p.m.–4:00 p.m. Summer hours are Monday through Saturday, 9:00 a.m.–5:00 p.m.; Sunday 1:00 p.m.–5:00 p.m.

Shelby Park, 20th Street South and Shelby Avenue, Nashville, TN 37219

Starwood Amphitheater, 3839 Murfreesboro Road, Antioch, TN 37013; (615) 641-5800. Season runs from the end of April to the beginning of October

 See inside Ryman Auditorium.

Tennessee Performing Arts Center, 505 Deaderick Street, Nashville, TN 37219; (615) 244-4878.

Tennessee State Capitol, Charlotte Avenue and Seventh Avenue, Nashville, TN 37219-5081; (615) 741-1621. Tours Monday through Friday several times a day. Call ahead if there are five or more in your group.

Tennessee State Department of Tourist Development, 320 Sixth Avenue North, Nashville, TN, 37219; (615) 741-2158.

Tennessee State Museum, 505 Deaderick Street, Nashville, TN 37213-1120; (615) 741-2692. Open Tuesday through Friday, 10:00 a.m.–5:00 p.m.; Sunday 1:00 p.m.–5:00 p.m. Closed Monday.

Uncle Bud's Catfish, four locations; (615) 790-1234. Open Monday through Thursday, 4:00 p.m.–9:00 p.m.; Friday and Saturday, 11:00 a.m.–10:00 p.m.; Sunday, 11:00 a.m.–9:00 p.m.

Union Station Hotel, 1001 Broadway, Nashville, TN 37203; (615) 726-1001 or (800) 331-2123.

Vanderbilt Commodores, (615) 322-GOLD. The Commodores play at Memorial Gym at Vanderbilt University. Their season runs November to March.

Warner Park Nature Center, 7311 Highway 100, Nashville, TN 37221; (615) 352-6299. Hours vary seasonally, so call ahead.

Wave Country Pool, 2320 Two Rivers Parkway; (615) 885-1052.

ANSWERS TO PUZZLES

page
7

```
S O U V E N I R S Q W E R T Y
A S D F G I C O L L E G E S R
N C N L S G A K Z X V B N B E
T H C O U N T R Y M U S I C S
R U T W Q W E R G Y C E L I T
D R S E M D F N B A N K S T A
E C S P G N U M H U I U Y E U
P H X S O P R Y L A N D M R R
A E N D U R H W Z B J L T F A
R S S E I S T R N F O R T S N
K O T B L K I S E U L Z A R T
S Y T H E A T E R L I M Q X S
```

page
11

```
J P A W X Z L P W L Z X J A Z W J
B Z J P J O Z J X A Z W R W D Z P
W P Z T X W H Z W P E X J W Z X J
X N X P A J P W S P H P Z X V W X
Z I W P X L W X Z X L P W X Z E W
T X R X X O Q W L L W X P E W Z Y
```

Hidden message:

ALL ABOARD THE NASHVILLE TROLLEY

page
17

page
19

page
21

ACROSS

2. ISLANDS
4. GO
6. GARDENS
7. BOY
8. ENGLISH

DOWN

1. FLOWERS
2. IN
3. SIGNS
5. HERB
6. GROVE

page
23

SHINGLES

POST

SHAPE

BLANKET

BIRDS

BRANCHES

DOOR

HEARTS

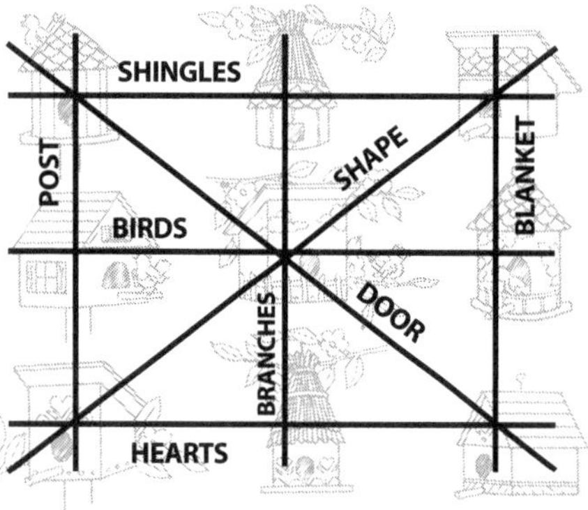

page
25

page
31

page
35

page
41

page
43

page
45

page
47

page
49

Hidden message: NASHVILLE, TENNESSEE

page
55

page
57

page
59

page
61

page
63

page
73

ACROSS

2. VILLAGE
5. BOLD
7. WEAPONS
8. QUILTS

DOWN

1. CIVIL WAR
3. LOG
4. GO
6. FOSSILS
7. WELL

page
75

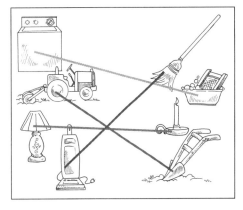

page
77

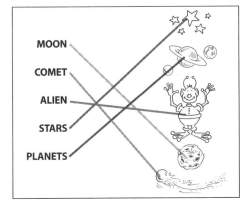

page
79

page
87

page
89

page
91

page
93

page
95

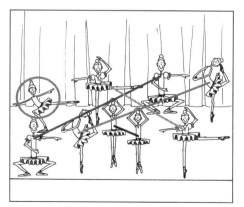

page
97

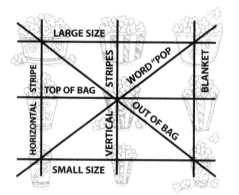

page
105

ACROSS

1. SODA SHOP
4. DINER
6. EAST
8. TABLE
9. SERVE

DOWN

1. SUNDAES
2. PLEASE
3. BEST
5. TIME
7. SHAKE

page
107

page
109

GEOGRAPHICAL INDEX

INDEX

PHOTO CREDITS

You'll Feel Like a Local when You Travel with Guides from John Muir Publications

CiTY·SMaRT™ GUIDEBOOKS

Pick one for your favorite city: *Albuquerque, Anchorage, Austin, Calgary, Cincinnati, Cleveland, Denver, Indianapolis, Kansas City, Memphis, Milwaukee, Minneapolis/St. Paul, Nashville, Portland, Richmond, San Antonio, St. Louis, Tampa/St. Petersburg*

Guides for kids 6 to 10 years old about what to do, where to go, and how to have fun in: *Atlanta, Austin, Boston, Chicago, Cleveland, Denver, Indianapolis, Kansas City, Miami, Milwaukee, Minneapolis/St. Paul, Nashville, Portland, San Francisco, Seattle, Washington D.C.*

TRAVEL✦SMART™

Trip planners with select recommendations to: *Alaska, American Southwest, Carolinas, Colorado, Deep South, Eastern Canada, Florida Gulf Coast, Hawaii, Kentucky/Tennessee, Michigan, Minnesota/Wisconsin, Montana/Wyoming/Idaho, New England, New York State, Northern California, Ohio, Pacific Northwest, South Florida and the Keys, Southern California, Texas, Western Canada*

Rick Steves' GUIDES

See *Europe Through the Back Door* and take along country guides to: *France, Belgium & the Netherlands; Germany, Austria & Switzerland; Great Britain & Ireland; Italy; Russia & the Baltics; Scandinavia; Spain & Portugal;* or the *Best of Europe*

ADVENTURES IN NATURE

Plan your next adventure in: *Alaska, Belize, Guatemala, Honduras*

JMP travel guides are available at your favorite bookstores. For a FREE catalog or to place a mail order, call: 800-888-7504.

John Muir Publications ✦ P.O. Box 613 ✦ Santa Fe, NM 87504

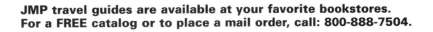

Cater to Your Interests on Your Next Vacation

The 100 Best Small Art Towns in America, 2nd edition
Where to Discover Creative People, Fresh Air, and Affordable Living
U.S. $15.95, Canada $22.50

The Big Book of Adventure Travel, 2nd edition
Profiles more than 400 great escapes to all corners of the world
U.S. $17.95, Canada $25.50

Cross-Country Ski Vacations
A Guide to the Best Resorts, Lodges, and Groomed Trails in North America
U.S. $15.95, Canada $22.50

Gene Kilgore's Ranch Vacations, 4th edition
The Complete Guide to Guest Resorts, Fly-Fishing, and Cross-Country Skiing Ranches
U.S. $22.95, Canada $32.50

Indian America, 4th edition
A Traveler's Companion to more than 300 Indian tribes in the United States
U.S. $18.95, Canada $26.75

Saddle Up!
A Guide to Planning the Perfect Horseback Vacation
U.S. $14.95, Canada $20.95

Watch It Made in the U.S.A., 2nd edition
A Visitor's Guide to the Companies That Make Your Favorite Products
U.S. $17.95, Canada $25.50

The World Awaits
A Comprehensive Guide to Extended Backpack Travel
U.S. $16.95, Canada $23.95

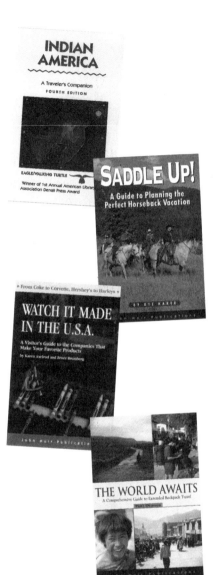

**JMP travel guides are available at your favorite bookstores.
For a FREE catalog or to place a mail order, call: 800-888-7504.**

John Muir Publications ◆ P.O. Box 613 ◆ Santa Fe, NM 87504

Cheekwood
1200 Forrest Park Drive
Nashville, TN 37205
615-356-8000

$4.00 VALUE!

Expires 3/15/2000

Valid for $1.00 off adult or children admission for up to four people. Not valid during Trees of Christmas.

**KIDDING AROUND®
NASHVILLE**

Cumberland Science Museum
800 Fort Negley Boulevard
Nashville, TN 37203
615-862-5160

$4.50 VALUE!

Expires 3/15/2000

Buy one adult admission and receive one child's admission free. Not valid with other discounts.

**KIDDING AROUND®
NASHVILLE**

Nashville Children's Theater
724 Second Avenue South
Nashville, TN 37210
615-254-9103

$6.00 VALUE!

Expires 3/15/2000

Valid for $1.50 off regular prices for up to four people. Subject to availability.

**KIDDING AROUND®
NASHVILLE**

Nashville Toy Museum
2613 McGavock Pike
Nashville, TN 37214
615-883-8870

KIDS FREE!

Expires 3/15/2000

Up to five kids free when accompanied by one paid adult.

**KIDDING AROUND®
NASHVILLE**

Country Music Hall of Fame & Museum
4 Music Square East
Nashville, TN 37203
615-255-5333

$1.00 VALUE!

Expires 3/15/2000

Valid for $1 off one child's admission with one paid adult.

**KIDDING AROUND®
NASHVILLE**

Sam Davis Home
1399 Sam Davis Road
Smyrna, TN 37167
615-459-2341

$5.00 VALUE!

Expires 3/15/2000

Buy one adult admission and receive two children's admissions free.

**KIDDING AROUND®
NASHVILLE**

Belmont Mansion

1900 Belmont Boulevard
Nashville, TN 37212
615-460-5459

$2.00 VALUE!

Expires 3/15/2000

**Valid for one free child admission with
one paid adult.**

KIDDING AROUND®
NASHVILLE

Wave Country

Two Rivers Parkway
at Briley Parkway
Nashville, TN
615-885-1092

$5.00 VALUE!

Expires 3/15/2000

**Buy one admission and receive a second
admission of equal or lesser value at no cost.**

KIDDING AROUND®
NASHVILLE

Nashville Zoo

I-24 West to Exit 31
615-746-3449
www.nashvillezoo.org

$4.00 VALUE!

Expires 3/15/2000

**One child free with each paid adult.
Not valid with other discounts.**

KIDDING AROUND®
NASHVILLE

Grand Old Golf

2444 Music Valley Drive
Nashville, TN 37214
615-871-4701

UP TO $2.00 VALUE!

Expires 3/15/2000

**Valid for $1 off one round of golf. Limit two people.
Not valid Friday or Saturday after 7:00 p.m.**

KIDDING AROUND®
NASHVILLE

Nashville Metros
Professional Soccer

Columbia Soccer Stadium
Harding Place, 1 mile east of I-24 at Exit 56
615-771-8200   www.nashville-metros.com

$4.00 VALUE!

Expires 3/15/2000

**Buy one adult ticket to any home game
and get one child's ticket free.**

KIDDING AROUND®
NASHVILLE

Vanderbilt
Commodores

McGugin Center at Vanderbilt University
2601 Jess Neely Drive, Nashville,
TN 37212   615-322-GOLD

$50.00 VALUE!

Expires 3/15/2000

**Buy one baseball season pass and get a
second season pass free!**

KIDDING AROUND®
NASHVILLE